THE HIDDEN IRELAND
Reassessment of a Concept

Essays and Texts in Cultural History I

THE HIDDEN IRELAND
Reassessment of a Concept

Louis M. Cullen

THE LILLIPUT PRESS
1988

First published in 1988 by
THE LILLIPUT PRESS LTD
Gigginstown, Mullingar,
Co. Westmeath, Ireland

British Library Cataloguing in Publication Data
Cullen, L. M. (Louis Michael), *1932*
The hidden Ireland: reassessment of a concept.
1.   Poetry in Irish, 1700-1850. Criticism
I.   Title
891.6'213'09

ISBN 0 946640 31 9

Acknowledgments
The essay is reprinted with kind permission of the editors of
Studia Hibernica, St Patrick's College, Dublin 9.
This book is published with financial assistance from
The Arts Council/An Chomhairle Ealaíon, Ireland.

Series editor: W. J. Mc Cormack

Cover design by Jarlath Hayes
Typeset by Redsetter Ltd of Dublin
Printed by Billings & Sons Ltd of Worcester, England.

Contents

Editor's Preface

This new series called ETCH, Essays and Texts in Cultural History, fills the gap between short articles in obscure journals and lengthy books at inflated prices. The field is the cultural history of Ireland in the broadest sense, including both work in Gaelic and English, non-literary material, and foreign commentary on Irish culture. The series includes essays originally commissioned, reprints of valuable items from the past, translations . . . indeed any kind of material which can increase our awareness of cultural history within Ireland, cultural history as it affects Ireland. W. J. Mc Cormack's *The Battle of the Books: Two Decades of Irish Cultural Debate* (Lilliput, 1986) can be regarded as the prototype of the series.

ETCH I – Louis Cullen's analysis of eighteenth-century Gaelic poetry, first published in *Studia Hibernica* in 1969, is a sustained critique of Daniel Corkery's notion of a 'hidden Ireland'. For over sixty years Corkery, whose book *The Hidden Ireland* was issued in 1925, has been a powerful influence in the debates surrounding Irish nationalism, its relation to the Gaelic language and to literature generally, and – more recently – in the controversies raised by the Field Day pamphlets. Where Corkery generalized from his reading of certain Munster poets to suggest an unproblematic national identity preserved in times of repression and deprivation, Cullen applies a unique combination of skills – of the economic historian and the chronicler of differentiated cultural groups – to advance a dissenting interpretation of the poetry and of the highly diverse Irish eighteenth century. The relevance of this argument today can hardly be exaggerated, as younger scholars reassess 'Georgian Ireland' or debate rival definitions of 'Protestant ascendancy'. Theatre audiences for Brian Friel's *Translations* and supporters of the revival of the Gaelic language will equally benefit from this provocative, well-informed and timely argument.

For the convenience of readers who have no knowledge of Gaelic, this edition of Professor Cullen's essay includes English prose translations of his copious quotations from the original literature. These have been prepared by Máirín Ní Dhonnchadha.

THE HIDDEN IRELAND
Reassessment of a Concept

I

The concept of a 'hidden Ireland' is now long established as an aspect of the interpretation of the eighteenth-century economic and social history of Ireland. The term is Daniel Corkery's, and since its first publication in 1925 his book of this title has run through four impressions and is now in paperback as well. Concept and book have both been influential. For Corkery, the hidden Ireland was 'that side of Irish life, the Gaelic side, which to him [Lecky] and his authorities was dark'[1] So far the concept would seem to suggest simply a corrective to Lecky's *History of Ireland in the eighteenth century* or a reminder that there were sources on which Lecky did not draw at all. But in Corkery's view the consequences of using the sources which were inaccessible to Lecky were not only significant but sweeping; they would alter Lecky's picture: 'We shall make on for thresholds that they [the historians, Lecky especially] never crossed over, in hope that what we shall further discover will not only complete the picture they have given, but frankly alter it . . .' (p. 5). Thus, while Corkery's book was first and foremost a literary argument based on literary sources, it was also, and was so regarded by Corkery, an historical work based on what Corkery described as a 'body of literature, almost all of which may be spoken of as explicitly or implicitly historical' (p. x). The success of Corkery's book has had a substantial impact on the understanding of the eighteenth century in Ireland. His concept of a hidden Ireland was in practice more than a merely cultural one: subsequent use of the term by literary men and historians alike has tended to be even less qualified.

An essential aspect of Corkery's theme was that Gaelic literature mirrored the outlook of the people. Indeed, he even goes so far as to intimate that the outlook of the people depended on their literature, 'the national life . . . being bound together by a national literature, depending indeed for its existence on that literature' (p. 95). Literature held the key to their outlook: his own 'immediate task is to show that Lecky presents us, for all his industry and learning, with only a body that is dead and ripe for burial ... To that Hidden Ireland of the Gaels, then, we turn our faces' (pp. 3-4). What the literature—the poetry—expressed was the fact that 'for two whole centuries our people were, we may say, down in the trenches, suffering so deeply that they sometimes cried out that God had forsaken them: their souls were therefore quick with such sensations as must find utterance in poetry or none' (p. 95). Continuity of outlook was marked: while Corkery recognised the aristocratic basis of the earlier poetry, 'tutoring years' in time made the ordinary people 'the residuary legatees of all the culture of the Gaelic ages' (p. 168). The poetry of the eighteenth century testifies to growing oppression: 'indeed, it may be that the vast distress in striking it quickened that soul into a new urgency of declaring itself, of uttering its cry' (p .95). Corkery's conclusion was that the cultural situation which he postulated had wide implications for Lecky and the historians: 'from his own pages one would never feel that the soul of the Gael is one of the more enduring features of our national life. Yet this very fact becomes daily more evident, and all future historians will more and more have to wrestle with it' (p. vii). Quoting Stopford Brooke's view that three elements could be found in poetry by Irishmen in the English tongue—nationality, religion, rebellion—Corkery wrote: 'now, one goes only a little way into the Irish poetry of the eighteenth century when one comes on the same three notes, the same, yet how vastly different! How much deeper, louder, stronger, fiercer!' (p. ix).

Had Corkery confined himself to making a purely intellectual or cultural case, his argument might have been stronger. But in his book the thesis that continuity can be traced from the cultural background to the political arena appears to be explicit: 'many years had to go by before they learned, out of a thousand experiences, that, outlawed and all as they were, they could still by combination resist oppression and exert influence, that they were indeed the historic Irish nation, that they would grow and be heard' (p. 168). This assumed continuity emerges strongly when he asserts: 'if instead of backwards we go forward twenty years from 1740 we are entering the period of Whiteboyism—evidence enough that the sufferings had come to a head and broken out' (p. 18). Here the Whiteboy Movement is regarded as a fulfilment of the outlook which he attributed to the poetry. At several points in Corkery's book the years around 1760 seem to be regarded as marking a transition from aristocratic to democratic, from bad to worse in terms of the degree of oppression, from poetic expression to organized resistance.

A distinctive intellectual outlook with its own growing political overtones is therefore the first aspect of Corkery's thesis. This feature, however, would not make sense except within the context of his second general assumption—that the eighteenth-century Gaelic environment was one of oppression, economic, political, religious. Corkery wrote: 'such, then, was in general the face of Ireland, such, more particularly, the face of Irish Ireland—that hidden land whose story has never been told. Poverty was its only wear—poverty in the town, the cabin, the person, the gear, the landscape. Civic life was not only broken, but wiped away. Institutions, and the public edifices, ceremonies, arts into which the institutional blossoms in home-centred countries, had ceased to exist. Life did no more than just crawl along, without enough to eat, unclothed, fever-stricken, slow . . .' (pp. 22-3). Conditions were continuously dark, similar throughout the century to the famine years of 1740-41: 'If we move either backward or forward from this midmost period of 1740, things are found to be no better' (p. 17). In fact, according to Corkery, things got much worse as the century progressed. After 1760 'Ireland began to be envisaged as England's feeding ground of the future . . . Then followed huge clearances . . . the result of all was that herds of dispossessed human beings, as well as the herds of beasts, began to darken the roads' (p. 25). The picture painted is one of unrelieved misery. 'Famine overtakes famine, or the people are cleared from the land to make room for bullocks' (p. 159), Corkery asserted. The land-system itself is presented as oppressive without qualification: 'there was no trick of squeezing money or value out of their tenants at will that these creatures [landlords] did not know and make use of' (p. 24). In Corkery's account of Irish history, there is a close connection between the outlook of the people and the economic and social conditions as he sees them. Not only that, but the accelerating deterioration of social conditions around 1760, which he claims to have occurred, is closely associated with the popular realization that 'they were indeed the historic Irish nation'. As already pointed out, Corkery saw in the Whiteboyism of the 1760s and later the background to what he regarded as the quickening of 'that soul into a new urgency of declaring itself, of uttering its cry'. The conjuncture at this time assumed by Corkery of the two themes—an outlook coloured by oppression and a dark economic and social environment—explains the significance which he saw in Eoghan Ruadh Ó Súilleabháin, the account of whom constitutes the longest chapter in the book. Ó Súilleabháin sprang from the same school of poetry as Ó Rathaile had sprung from at an earlier date—that of Sliabh Luachra (p. 193), and at the same time he was 'as democratic in feeling as Ó Rathaile was aristocratic' (p. 168). For Corkery, Ó Súilleabháin drew on the continuity of Irish culture and at the same time represented a democratic outlook, reflecting what Corkery saw as the environment and attitudes of 1760.

The concept of a hidden Ireland was primarily a literary one. The only substantial criticism of Corkery has been literary. Yet the concept has been used as an historical interpretation not only by Corkery and other literary men, but by many historians. Apart from the validity or otherwise of Corkery's concept, the approach itself—the use of literary material as historical evidence—has considerable relevance to the historian's task of describing men and conditions as they were in their own times. Historians have often relied on Corkery's concept and his book, but, apart from incidental quotation they have rarely approached the contemporary literary evidence afresh. Yet it seems worth doing so, partly to see whether the hidden Ireland, as Corkery saw it, is an acceptable historical interpretation, partly as a tentative exploration of a more general issue debated among historians at present—whether and how should literary evidence be used in the course of historical enquiry. Several questions come to mind. Is Corkery's thesis acceptable? If it creates difficulties of acceptance, in what lie the difficulties, and how should the sources be interpreted? And if there are pitfalls in interpreting the literary sources, what light if any does poetry throw on attitudes and living conditions? In the Irish context this is perhaps an appropriate time to raise these questions. For a later century and for different literary materials, Professor Connell has raised them in an essay on Catholicism and marriage in nineteenth-century Ireland.[2] The emotional and emotive issues that surround this subject have however tended to deflect critical attention from an assessment of the approach which Professor Connell put forward in his essay.

An immediately obvious limitation in Corkery's concept is that the location of the hidden Ireland appears to be curiously elusive. Much of the book would suggest that it was limited to regions where big houses with an Irish culture survived. It is frequently suggested in the book that it was to be found in bogs, hills or mountains (pp. 4, 8, 185). Corkery even wrote that 'if that period was hard on the poor who tilled . . . the golden soils of central Ireland, we may conceive how it must have been with the Gaels, whose only portion was rock and bog and windswept seashore' (p. 9). Corkery states elsewhere in the book that 'the hidden Ireland was in a sense coterminous with Ireland itself, bounded only by the same four seas' (p. 5). He speaks of 'the state of Catholic Ireland in the eighteenth century' (p. 27), and of 'the facts here gathered being the commonplaces of the social history of eighteenth century Ireland' (p. 23). At other points, Corkery seems to be writing of 'Catholic Munster' (p. 12)—the subtitle of the book is of course 'a study of Gaelic Munster in the eighteenth century'—but even this definition is a good deal wider than the more precise locations hinted at in references to mountain, bog and sea. This defect in Corkery's concept however he inherited from other sources which inspired his approach. In a work of some length describing pre-Famine life in county Kerry which had a discernible influence on Corkery's account of social conditions in Munster, Father Dinneen wrote: 'ag trácht ar mhuinntir Chiarraidhe dhom tráchtaim ar mhuinntir na Mumhan ar fad'.[3] While Corkery may not have read any of James Anthony Froude's writings, he was certainly influenced by authors who had come under the direct or indirect impact of his writing. Froude's history of Ireland gave disproportionate attention to counties Cork and Kerry, and generalisations about social or economic conditions are often based on limited evidence relating to these regions.[4] His romantic involvement with the region is also displayed in his essay 'A fortnight in Kerry', and in his historical novel *The two chiefs of Dunboy*.[5]

The real weakness of the hidden-Ireland concept lies, however, not in its lack of geographical definition but in its origins. Corkery's achievement was to give a clear-cut title to a concept which already existed in fact. Far from the concept springing from a careful assessment of the historical or even literary evidence of the period, we must seek its origins in the complex character and outlook of James Anthony Froude. Froude was eager to prove that the obvious failure of the Union between Britain and Ireland was not in the nature of things, that difficulties before and after the Union lay in institutions rather than in national character. If institutions and law were right, harmony between Saxon and Celt could be achieved.[6] To emphasize the institutional character of the problem, he painted a dramatically dark picture of British policy, law and institutions relating to Ireland, his object consciously or unconsciously not being historical but one of showing how the English interest in Ireland could be preserved. His pursuit of this purpose produced an unqualified picture of havoc, oppression and poverty in Ireland. As far as the native Irish were concerned, 'the law had been their enemy, and therefore they were lawless. They could gain nothing by being industrious and therefore they were idle'.[7] This situation also made smuggling rife: 'the restrictions inflicted by English selfishness on Irish trade in the last century erected smuggling into patriotism'.[8] As for the land-system, 'the landlords were for the most part aliens in blood and aliens in religion. They represented conquest and confiscation, and they had gone on from generation to generation with an indifference to the welfare of the people which would not have been tolerated in England and Scotland'.[9] At the same time, his picture of English influence on Irish society was made still more condemnatory by his view of bright prospects which had been frustrated. First of all, the Irish character was not naturally flawed; it was only vitiated by a defective policy and laws. His view of the Irish, odd though it was, was in fact suffused with a sympathy and with a belief in a potential which could be made fruitful in the right circumstances under a Union :'when all is said, Ireland is still the most beautiful island in the world, and the Irish themselves, though their temperament is ill-matched to ours, are still among the most interesting of peoples'.[10] Secondly, he professed to see a real economic potential gone to waste, its extent adding to the gravity of the charges laid at the door of institutions. A traveller in 1802, according to Froude, 'would have seen three-quarters of a country, richer naturally than Scotland, as rich as the best parts of England, lying a wilderness, dotted with potato gardens'.[11] Of the valleys of Kerry, Froude thought that they 'would support, if properly tilled, at least twice their present population with ease'.[12] Thirdly, his remarks, though written from a vastly different point of view, accorded in many ways with political prejudices and nationalist beliefs. Froude's assertion that 'the heart of the matter lies in the land . . . under English agent and Irish middleman, the peasantry have been robbed; and it has been this systematic plunder which has deprived them of the natural motive to exertion . . .'[13] was bound to have an appeal during the period of the land war. Statements such as 'England deserves what has come upon her'[14] and 'I confess that had I been myself expelled from my holding by a landlord's crowbar, I should not have felt particularly loving towards the Government that allowed it',[15] are not only sweeping, but help to account for the fact recently pointed out by Mr Donal MacCartney[16] that Froude had a greater appeal for extreme nationalists than for more moderate opinion.

Froude's influence on Irish historiography was enormous. He was the real originator of the hidden-Ireland concept. Lecky's *History of Ireland in the eighteenth century* was a response to issues raised by Froude. As such it necessarily covered the same ground, and when he did not conflict with Froude, Lecky's account simply confirmed Froude's and with the weight of more obviously detached scholarship. The works of Froude and more particularly Lecky powerfully coloured the first economic histories of Ireland.[17] Apart from detail, none of them appears to advance beyond the framework which emerged in the writings of Lecky and Froude. The rise of the Gaelic League and later of Sinn Féin led to a heightened national conciousness. Identifying certain elements in the poetry of the eighteenth century, it quickly read into those elements its own preoccupations. Hyde, for instance, writing of Raftery, stated: 'ach nuair tá fhios againn go raibh an dall so 'na chumhacht in san tír, ag gríosughadh na ndaoine a n-aghaidh na ndeachmhuidhe agus gá mbrostughadh a n-aghaidh a namhad, má's olc maith a chuid abhrán is fiú a gcruinniughadh ar a shon sin féin'.[18] Here the political preoccupation seems obvious. Dinneen, too, tended to read into the poetry of the eighteenh century the interests created by the cultural and political situation in modern Ireland: 'The sense of national life crushed under the yoke of oppression, the hankering after national freedom and religious equality . . . are reflected in the writings of the chief bards of that period.'[19] He speaks of Eoghan Ruadh Ó Súilleabháin's 'mission, which was an eternal protest against the tyranny of the English and a kindling of the minds of the people into courage and hope'.[20] The impact of the cultural and linguistic renaissance on Dinneen's outlook seems strong: 'the events of recent years have done something to dissipate that foul atmosphere which young and old, learned and unlearned have so long been breathing, and we are gradually getting a clearer vision of the great figures that adorned the past and whose spirit of song nerved every fibre of the nation in its hour of supreme struggle. Viewed through a clearer air the eighteenth century is a glorious epoch in Irish history'.[21]

The influence of Dinneen on Corkery is decisive. Dinneen's indefatigable industry, with no less than seven volumes of edited poetry to its credit,[22] had made Munster poetry better known and more accessible than that of the other provinces. Dinneen's work explains why Corkery attempted his study, and why it was confined to Munster. Although Froude must be regarded as the effective creator of the hidden-Ireland concept, there is no evidence in Corkery's book that he had read Froude. If he had read Froude at all and if he had followed Lecky's commentary on Froude's case, it would seem unlikely that Mícheál Coimín's abduction of a young lady could be attributed to the poet's Protestantism, and that Corkery could have asserted that 'hearing of these incidents, we would be perplexed if we did not know of his different station in life: though a Gael, he could afford to have his fling, even to the breaking of the law' (pp. 291-2). This adds support to the case for the preponderant influence of Dinneen on the shaping of the *Hidden Ireland.*

There are several points which give more detailed substance to this assertion. First, Dinneen's picture of Irish life before the Famine, as I have already mentioned, had a discernible role in shaping Corkery's picture of the economic and social environment. Secondly, Dinneen had already described the essence of the hidden-Ireland theme. Writing of the Maigue poets, he had said:

> The poems in question, though barren as regards formal fact, tell us the history of the inner life of the people as no other documents can. State papers, photographs, paintings, wills, deeds, private letters of public personages, such records as these have their value in interpreting for us the character of a people at a given period of their historical development, but they have not the power of introducing us to the inner sanctum of the people's life where their emotions well forth in all their native vigour. [23]

Corkery has not said it better or more succinctly. Thirdly, Corkery's high regard for the poetic merit of Eoghan Ruadh Ó Súilleabháin and for his place in the hidden Ireland of Munster seems to have been taken from Dinneen. 'He is, nevertheless, the literary glory of his country,' [24] Dinneen had claimed. Fourthly, the idea that the Gaelic poets were peasants had been enounced by Dinneen: 'the poets themselves, in spite of the light of genius that shone in their souls, had often to lead a life of drudgery, such as is the lot of the labourer or the tradesman'. [25] Formalised by Corkery's pen, the concept becomes a confining one. To the historian it seems to stereotype people, motivations, situations. It has even much of the remoteness that is sometimes associated with Anglo-Irish writers like Somerville and Ross. Corkery was imposing a pattern on the eighteenth century rather than describing it.

II

Much of the poetry of the eighteenth century has as its theme the downfall and oppression of the Gael. However, aristocratic lamentations about the dispossession of landed families do not themselves imply genuine oppression, even before we allow for poetic convention, still less when we allow for poetic convention of expression. While the aristocratic basis of early Munster poets hardly needs stressing, it can be detected in later poetry as well. Ó Tuama lamented 'uaisle Gaedheal fá chruadh smacht ghéar'; [26] Mac Gearailt wrote: 'mo chás! mo nuar! na h-uaisle ar fán go faon'. [27] Although Corkery had claimed Ó Súilleabháin to be 'as democratic in feeling as Ó Rathaile was aristocratic' Ó Súilleabháin appears to be very much in the tradition of the earlier poets. In *Ag taisteal na sléibhthe dhom*, for instance, he bewailed

> Sliocht Chaisil i ndaor-bhroid fá ard chíos
> Ag gallaibh an Bhéarla do shealbhuigh aol-bhrogh
> Is fearann gach éinne dar áirmhigheas.[28]

In the north almost one-third of Art Mac Cubhthaigh's poems lamented the downfall of the O'Neills. A lesser poet, Uilliam Ó Maoil Chiaráin lamented the O'Reilly family in Meath as well:

> Ach tá an réim seo le Gallaí
> Ó d'imthigh Raghailligh agus Clanna Néill uainn.[29]

References to rents are largely general and conventional. What was resented was not rent in itself but its payment to foreigners who had replaced the old nobility. Mac Cubhthaigh complained of 'na tíortha ag osnaigh faoi léan ar léagsaí'.[30] Here the very leases are resented: they were the legal expression of the new system. But in themselves leases, far from denoting poverty, were regarded as a sign of security and comfort by contemporaries. A later and less exalted Ulster poet, Peadar Ó Doirnín, in *Sabha Nic Oireachtaigh*, actually writes:

> Níl aon duine bocht i muinín cúpla mart
> Nach dtabharfaidh mé bearach is féar dó,
> Nó go gcuinneochaidh siad stoc is maoin mhór ar cnoc
> Is go bhfaighidh siad téarma is léagsaí.[31]

Resentment of rents, evident in the Munster poetry, is not to be taken as evidence of the oppressive character of such rents, but as a sign of the poets' customary yearning for the old Gaelic system, or as Eoghan Ruadh Ó Súilleabháin expressed it:

> go mbeidh aicme na nGaedheal san réim is aoirde
> ina bhfearannaibh féin gan aon rud cíosa.[32]

What was resented was not rent itself, but the fact that it was being paid, in the estimate of the poets, to the wrong people. In *Moladh Shéamuis Pluincéad* Mac Cubhthaigh had referred nostalgically to:

> Den chaomh choill sin Séamus ó fhréimh:
> do dhúthchas na ndaoine a mbéadh dúitheacha is tíortha
> ag umhlú faoi chíos dóibh gan díombuadh go léir.[33]

9

The degree of alienation suggested by the *aisling* should not be exaggerated. Aristocratic in its inspiration and in its oft-expressed hope for the restoration of the Gaelic lords, it affords no concrete evidence of social oppression. Political alienation it may suggest, but even this is difficult to assess from the *aislings* and from Jacobite poetry generally. Moreover, many well-to-do Catholics had dissociated themselves from sympathy for the Stuart cause at a rather early date. In the 1730s Charles O'Connor of Belanagare had written:

As for the Pretender, I neither like nor detest his cause. I am of the opinion the affairs of this Kingdom may be well enough administered with or without his presiding over them; and as the present disposition runs, I believe the Government would be safer in any other hands than his.[34]

The poets, too, rapidly lost faith in the Stuart cause. Ó Doirnín's *Tá bearád i Londain* has been described as a send-up of the *aisling* genre.[35] Piaras Mac Gearailt who had written many *aislings* wrote in 1769 of one of his own compositions: 'is iomdha glór díomhaoin i gceann an té a chom an t-amhrán so, 's go bhfóire Dia air gan chiall'.[36] Of another poet's effort—*An t-aodhaire óg*—he wrote: 'go dtugaidh Dia ciall do'n leath-éarla dúirt an duanóg so, ó's é Liam Inglis é'.[37] Yet all Eoghan Ruadh Ó Súilleabháin's *aisling* poems come from a later date. On at least two occasions, Ó Súilleabháin himself appears to indicate that the *aisling* was not to be taken seriously. In *Saxaibh na séad*, the poet declared:

Is eagal liom féin a réilteann lonnrach
Gur reacaireacht bhréag an scéal so thionnscnais[38] . . .

Almost identical words appear in *Ar maidin indé cois cé*.[39] It would appear hard not to agree with Traolach Ó Raithbheartaigh when he says 'gur fanntaisidheacht agus nach mothú a bhí ar siubhal ag an fhile', and 'ní shílim go bhfuil náisiúntacht ar bith ionnta.'[40]. It would of course be possible to argue—as Professor Ó Tuama does—that one should not expect realism in an *aisling* and that behind the fantasy the poet was expressing the popular hope for national salvation: 'Cén rí eile, san 18ú haois in Éirinn, is fearr a mhúsclódh dóchas an tslánaithe in aigne an phobail'.[41] I am not sure, however, that this view is tenable. Rake though he was, it is clear that Ó Súilleabháin was received in circles where the old culture and its poetic forms were still practised. He was no ordinary *spailpín*, nor in fact did he regard himself as one. This seems all the more likely when we recall that Ó Súilleabháin was not the democrat in aspirations that Corkery suggests he was. The poems represented composition on themes and in a form which had been traditional before his time. The *aisling* was a literary form; not a message for the people. In *Saxaibh na séad*, for instance, the poet actually says: 'aithris mo scéal don éigse ag baile'.[42]

While the poetry suggests alienation, and may even have helped to keep a feeling of alienation alive, it does not constitute evidence of the existence of a community, oppressed economically or socially. Moreover, in the Connacht poetry and, after the early poetry, in Ulster as well, the aristocratic themes seem to be absent. In any event, even in the case of the Munster poetry, a link of continuity does not appear to exist between the aristocratic feeling expressed in the early poetry and the social unrest which emerged here and there after 1760. This unrest was as a rule concerned with very specific grievances such as county cesses, enclosure, tithes, competition for land among peasants, resentment of the outsider who took land when local men also sought it.

A rather interesting case, however, is the poetry of Máire Bhuidhe Ní Laoghaire, because in her poetry imitation of earlier traditions was still evident. In *Ar leacain na gréine*, there is reference in the manner of the *aisling* to help from Laoiseach and from the Spaniards, despite the fact that the help expected was coming from republican France. The tone of the poetry, however, is distinctly more plebeian. The earlier poets had generally referred to freedom from rent as a symbol of the restoration of land to its rightful owners. Here one of the themes of earlier Munster poetry—that land will be free from rent—has lost its aristocratic association, and is linked in a novel fashion to the hope of material improvement:

> Beidh talamh gan chíos gan íoc
> gan cháin is gan pléidhe
> Beidh cruithneacht is im is saill
> ar an gclár againn féin.[43]

A similar theme emerges a little later in the Connacht poem *Na Buachaillí Bána*,[44] which written by or for people poorer than the cattle-owning families such as Máire Bhuidhe's, contemplates the destruction of cattle stocks:

11

Cia'n bhrí an chluiche seo go dtagaidh 'n Spáinneach
'S imtheochaidh 'n Parliament ó chumhacht an rí,
Seo é 'n imirc a bhfuighmuid sásadh
Béidh an talamh bán againn ar bheagán cíos'.

Ag teacht an tséasúir déanfaimid sléuchta
Marbhóchamuid céad agus dá mhíle bó,
Béidh buailí Shasan le beagán géimnighe
Ag teacht an tséasúir má bhíonn muid beo.
Béidh leathar fáirsing ag na gréasaibh Gaedealach'
'S ní iarrfamuid péire orrtha níos lugha ná coróin
Béidh bróga againn-ne gan Dia dá méadughadh
'S ní íosfamuid béile níos mó gan feoil.

This theme also expresses a feeling that may have been present in the occasional bouts of cattle houghing or maiming which occurred in well-defined areas, including Galway, from an early date. One may find an echo of this attitude also in a fairly early Ulster poem, *Cathal Mhac Aoidh*, that of a highwayman or cattle thief:

Thug siad a mbréag, ní gadaí mé fhéin,
Ar son mé bheith éadtrom, earraideach, baoth,
'S dá mbainfinn luach éadaigh do bhodaigh an Bhéarla
Cé bheadh 'na dhéidh ar Chathal Mhac Aoidh.

Referring to one of the 'bodaigh an Bhéarla', Uilliam Piaras, he stated:

Is aoibhinn 's is códha a gheobhainn-se an t-eolas
Ar fud a chuid bó dá dhorcha an oidhch'.[45]

The theme, however, is very rare in the poetry of all the provinces, and absent apparently from Munster poetry. Not only was much of the poetry in practice and inspiration imitative of aristocratic examples or aspirations, but too many Catholics owned, as we shall see, at least some property, to make acceptance of such themes welcome or general. In any event poetry of humbler origin or inspiration was often less critical of or concerned with rents than the more aristocratic poetry or poetry such as Máire Bhuidhe Ní Laoghaire's which was influenced by such traditions. Compare, for instance, the practical realism of the line in *Na Buachaillí Bána*: 'Beidh an talamh bán againn ar bheagán cíos' with Máire Bhuidhe Ní Laoghaire's more sweeping aspiration: 'Beidh talamh gan chíos, gaň íoc, gan cháin is gan pléidhe', which hearkens back to more aristocratic pretensions.

What one does find however in much early nineteenth-century poetry in Connacht and in Munster is a bitter sectarianism for which there does not appear to be a parallel in the previous century. Sectarian sentiment there had been of course in eighteenth-century poetry. But it often arose in the context of the aristocratic concern with the replacement of the old landed class by a new one, English and Protestant; strong or bitter though the language used was, the repetition of the theme in similar terms by the same or by successive poets suggests that its use was to a large extent conventional. Good feeling between Catholic and Protestant was not altogether uncommon in practice. Even Mac Cubhthaigh, though bitterly commenting on some of the changes, including those affecting religion, betrayed no evidence of sectarian feeling in commenting on the participation of a descendant of the O'Neills in the Oakboys in the 1760s.[46] Moreover, in a period when so many of the surviving Catholic landowners conformed, conversion to Protestantism was free from the abhorrence it often aroused in the nineteenth century. The poets' comments on their own change of religion reveal a wry sense of humour and even when they remained loyal to their new allegiance, they did not forego former friendships. Bitterness at a deep level over changes of religion, as reflected in the poetry, seems to be largely confined to changes by priests or brothers, and more especially where conversion was followed by ministry in the established church.[47] Sectarian bitterness as a divisive social and political force came only later. The religious tensions surrounding the foundation of the Orange Order in 1795, the real and imagined atrocities committed on both sides during '98 and government efforts in those years to exploit sectarian feeling to prevent alliance between religious groups, powerfully fed the forces of sectarian division.

The division split the landed class itself. Indeed, the contesting of elections by rival landed candidates of the 'Ascendancy' and of liberal outlook respectively helped to polarise division at local level and to perpetuate it. Sectarian feeling took its sharpest form during elections, as rival landlord groups of liberal and 'Ascendancy' outlook strove with one another. Catholic emancipation and the payment of tithes provided, after the first two decades, polarising-points for the sectarian feeling already widespread. At the same time as an aggressive ascendancy outlook developed, there was also an evangelical movement to catechise and convert Catholics. Coming at a time when sectarian feeling had become embittered, it often assumed, especially at local level, an importance altogether disproportionate to the resources or the success of the attempts. All these themes one can follow in the poetry of Raftery.[48] They crop up in other poetry as well, illustrating the pervasiveness of the sectarian feeling of the early nineteenth century. Before and after '98, fear of the Orangemen was widespread; much of the fear was irrational but, allied to the growing sectarian feeling on both sides and the highlighting of 'Ascendancy' bigotry in electoral clashes between its proponents and liberal landlords, it powerfully aided the spread of sectarian division. The *Prophecies of Pastorini*, foretelling conflict between Catholic and Protestant, and the final overwhelming of the latter, spread rapidly towards 1820 in the countryside. Anti-Orange feeling is said to have been a powerful factor in the founding of clubs of Ribbonmen.[49] Pastorini is quoted both by Máire Bhuidhe Ní Laoghaire and by Raftery. The form and depth of this bitterness are quite novel. In *Cath Chéim an Fhiaidh*, Máire Bhuidhe Ní Laoghaire, referring to Pastorini, stated:

> gurab é deir gach ughdar cruinn liom sara gcríochna siad deire
> an fhoghmhair
> Ins an leabhar so Pastorína go ndíolfaid as an bpóit.[50]

Again, in *Tá Gaedhil bhocht cráidhte*, she declares:

> Is é chuala ó fháidhibh go ndubhairt Naomh Seán linn
> Go raibh deire an chairde caithte leo
> 'S go dtiocfadh slaughter ar gach piara másach
> Nár ghéill don Pháis is do chaith an phóit.[51]

Time and time again Raftery turned to Pastorini or to St John and his 'revelation'. In *An Cíos Catoilceach*, he declared:

> Sgríobh Pastorini go dtiucfadh an bealach-sa
> Lá gach aon mhí go mbéadh cruinniugh' ins gach baile aca
> Ag Cluain-Meala béidh díbirt ar *New Lights* a's *Orangemen*,
> 'S i mBaile Locha Riach, 'seadh léigheadh a mbeath dhóibh.[52]

In *Bearnán Ristéard*, he declared:

> . . . sgríobh Pastoríní nach fada uainn an lá
> Go mbéidh Galla suaighte sínte gan duine le n-a gcaoineadh . . .
> Acht ó thosaigh Hannraoi a ghníomhartha tá Caitiolcaigh
> ar lár,

Acht béidh siad suas aríste tá an spás i bhfogus díobhtha
A mbéidh 'Orangemen' d'á spíonadh agus spíodóirí le fán.[53]

Even in *Seanchas na Sgeiche*, the same issue is brought up:

'S go ndeir San Seaghan in san 'revelation'
An naomhadh bliadhain fichead go mbéidh an sgór le
Gaedealaibh.[54]

This is a new theme. It did not universally divide peasant from landed class, because popular opinion often as conspicuously espoused one electoral side as it abhorred the other. Neither does it constitute an element of continuity from the preceding century.

One important aspect of this situation was a change in the relationship between Catholic clergymen and laity. Anti-clerical tones can be detected from time to time in the poetry of the eighteenth century. One finds them, for instance, in Art Mac Cubhthaigh's famous *Máire Chaoch*,[55] or in Peadar Ó Doirnín's *Tairngire Dhearscnaí*.[56] They are re-echoed more mildly on occasion in Eoghan Ruadh Ó Súilleabháin.[57] As Mr John A. Murphy has pointed out, anti-clerical feeling against their own clergy was often marked in Whiteboy unrest in the 1780s.[58] One should not make too much of the presence of anti-clerical feeling. Much eighteenth-century poetry especially that of the Maigue poets or of Seán na Ráithíneach Ó Murchadha reveals very friendly ties between poet and individual clergymen. This poetry does, however, suggest a greater equality between laymen and clergymen than was the case in the nineteenth century. It is of course to be remembered that these poets were not in fact quite the simple peasants that Corkery represents them to be, and that one can hardly compare the relationships suggested in their poems with those of parish clergy with their more modest parishioners. One can find in early nineteenth-century poetry a pronounced emphasis on following the lead of the clergy. The sectarian conflict may well have made closer the bonds between clergy and people, drawing both together under the leadership of the former.

In the manner in which it is usually formulated, the outlook postulated in the hidden-Ireland concept has to be examined closely. But, granted a distinctiveness in the poetry, it cannot be rejected altogether. Some of this distinctiveness, however, as the late Professor Gerard Murphy noted, was a survival of a medieval character.[59] It is doubtful whether it is helpful to label this as the 'hidden Ireland.' The uneven and often isolated character of this survival helps to account for the geographical ambivalence painfully evident in

Corkery's book.

Continuity in the hidden Ireland in the sense in which Corkery sees it also poses a problem. The assimilation by Corkery of the aristocratic concern about land settlement to later manifestations of unrest seems to make light of the problem. For one thing, it involves the assumption that there was an identity of outlook and interest among the Irish. This assumption must itself be seen in the light of the claim that Irish culture was homogeneous. Corkery spoke of 'the unity of mind between the Big House and the cabin' (p. 56). But this overlooks the social divisions which existed in Ireland. There were poor and well-to-do in Gaelic Ireland. Poetry, especially Munster poetry, and more particularly the aspirations expressed in Munster poetry, were those of the well-to-do. The outlook expressed in the early Munster and Ulster poetry is backward-looking: what is sought is restoration, not revolution. In this regard, reference is appropriate to the words of a recent historian looking at sixteenth and seventeenth-century unrest in Europe: 'how far can historians accustomed to look for *innovation* among revolutionaries, enter into the minds of men who themselves were obsessed by *renovation*—by the desire to return to old customs and privileges, and to an old order of society'.[60] To what extent did the ordinary people share these aspirations? They knew or sang the songs. But this does not prove that they shared the aspirations, or more accurately that the aspirations grew out of the problems or conditions of the ordinary people. Popular songs were based on older or more cultivated models. Their themes were imitative of ideals that did not grow out of peasant life at all. This is true even of something at first sight as intimate as love poetry. The ideals expressed in the love poetry of the eighteenth century seem amoral by the standards of peasant conduct at that time.[61] As Corkery himself stated of the popular songs of the period: 'they gave them welcome for the art that was in them than for the tidings' (p. 136).

What is evident in the poetry is a sense of separateness, a sense of identity and nationality stronger than sectional interests. If Corkery had simply stated that the poetry conveyed a strong sense of national identity, he could not have been contradicted. That the sense of identity, heightened by the struggle between the two races, fused sectional interests that might otherwise have proved divisive, seems incontrovertible. In particular, a ruling class, stripped of some of its privileges, is likely to have far more in common with its peasantry than a class which successfully preserves its position; the sense of defeat engulfed class differences. This seems to emerge in Arthur

Young's account of Charles O'Connor of Clonalis, descendant of
the high king: 'the common people pay him the greatest respect, and
send him presents of cattle etc., upon various occasions. They consider him as the prince of a people involved in one common ruin'.[62]
Professor Mac Cana has added: 'for as the Irish upper classes were
extirpated, much of their literature was forced down to the level of
the Gaelic speaking peasantry and became their exclusive patri-
mony'.[63] This is substantially true provided that we make allowance
for the decidedly aristocratic tone of much of the poetry written
even in the eighteenth century. For the poetry reflected the aspirations or the nostalgia of a landed or upper class reduced in circumstances. Of his visit to county Cork, Young had recorded: 'all the
poor people are Roman Catholics, and among them are the descendants of the old families who once possessed the country, of which
they still preserve the full memory, in so much that a gentleman's
labourer will regularly leave to his son, by will, his master's estate'.[64]
Young's statement is rather vague, the result of information acquired
at second hand. But the point of his statement is definite enough,
even if as we shall see later many of the inheritors of aristocratic
aspirations fared well enough in the economic conditions of the
eighteenth century, and hardly fused with the surrounding peasantry
to the point of becoming 'gentlemen's labourers'. Nevertheless, the
two classes intermingled to a degree. The ordinary people acquired
the cultural outlook which gives this period of popular literature in
Irish a particular richness and distinctiveness; they also absorbed
some of the resentments or aspirations revolving around the resettlement of land in Ireland in the second half of the seventeenth
century. What is not legitimate, however, is to assume, this process
having been allowed for, that the very terms of the poetry itself
constitute evidence of popular economic and social oppression.
Yet this is what is done: the tone of the poetry is taken as evidence
of social or economic conditions which make the existence of such
a corpus of poetry a phenomenon which has to be accounted for:
'A dhealúsaí a bhí an saol ba ait le duine go dtiocfadh aon saghas
filíochta chun cinn in aon chor'.[65] Such assumptions overlook the
aristocratic nature of much of the poetry, and of its conventions and
imagery. They also fail to take into account the real division which
existed in Gaelic Ireland, and the fact that the conventions of the
poetry, while they are indicative of some of the attitudes of the time,
obscure rather than illuminate the study of actual social and economic
conditions.

The continuity of Irish poetry or Irish attitudes as reflected in poetry in Irish is thus more complex than has usually been assumed. The continuity masks rather than cements social divisions. Moreover, the most outstanding feature of the poetry—and certainly the most outstanding element of continuity in it—is a sense of *racial* identity. It is indeed a similar situation to what Elliot found in his study of the European situation generally: 'whether the community was local or national, expressions of allegiance to it assumed the same form: a deep and instinctive antipathy to foreigners'.[66] The dislike of foreign intruders emerges strongly in the Gaelic poetry of the seventeenth and eighteenth centuries; it accounts for the most violent language in the poetry of the period; it, rather than religious animosity in its own right, lies behind the rather abstract antipathy to the Reformation and to the reformed churches. This sentiment is accompanied by a pride in the Gaelic race and by a heightened awareness of its antiquity. This racial sense existed well before 1700; it existed already in medieval Ireland, although modern historians, reacting understandably against some of the excessive claims by twentieth-century nationalists, have played it down too much. In the eighteenth century, it was as ever a potent force, exacerbated by the great upheavals of the seventeenth century and the memory of them. Some of the strength of the racial rivalry associated with this sense of identity comes through in sources not involved with Ireland at all. For instance, Sir James Lowther, writing from London to his agent in Whitehaven in 1745, stated: 'There are vast numbers of Irish papists and other disaffected people in this town who began to talk very imprudently after the defeat of Sir John Cope'.[67] The English vice-consul, in Corunna, referring repeatedly to the activites of the 'Irish clan' in his jurisdiction, spoke of 'our nation's inveterate enemies, the Irish'.[68] These circumstances are sufficient to account for the outlook expressed in the Irish poetry of the period. To seek a hidden Ireland to explain it is to underestimate its universality and force in Irish history and to attach too much attention to some of the features of the eighteenth-century social and economic scene, in so far as one can identify them at all from the Gaelic literature of the period.

III

The second aspect of the hidden-Ireland concept is the economic and social environment which has been claimed to be a distinctive one of poverty and oppression. The arguments put forward in support of this understanding of the situation may not unfairly be summarized in two points. First, there were few comparatively comfortable Catholics. Second, the land system was unjust and arbitrary. In particular, rents were crushing. Both points should be looked at in turn.

Corkery's case was essentially that, apart from a small number of big houses, there were few Catholics in comfortable circumstances. In fact, of course, even Corkery had to face the situation that Irish poetry itself does not consistently sustain this argument. For instance, he noted Seán Clárach Mac Domhnaill as 'a sort of gentleman farmer', dying in 1754 'before the Gaels had become utterly destitute' (p. 257). Apart from the few 'big houses' and some other exceptions for the first half of the century, poverty was general: 'Irish Ireland had become in the eighteenth century a peasant nation, harried and poverty-stricken with the cottier's smoky cabin for stronghold' (p. 30). The same problem arises for the second half of the century. Professor Ó Tuama has written: 'Ní minic a shamhlaítear uaisleacht ná compord leis an saol Gaelach san 18ú aois. Ar a shon sin, is fíor go raibh teaghlaigh thall is i bhfus ag maireachtaint sámh go maith fós'.[69] Corkery regarded the poets as peasants (p. 147), living in poverty: 'as each advanced from youth to manhood and from manhood to age, he became poorer and poorer; and as the century advanced from decade to decade, each new poet that comes into our ken is poorer than the last' (p. 156). What Corkery has done in effect is to take at their face value rhetorical references to their circumstance by the poets, which are general, conventional and imitative, and conveying what may be described as the aristocratic sense of loss or grievance at the revolution in land ownership. Not only is the case that the mass of Irishmen lived in abysmal poverty and oppression doubtful but the case that the poets themselves did so is unimpressive. Corkery, for instance, regarded Merriman and Mac Gearailt as living or dying in poverty (pp. 168, 239, 290). But there appears to be no evidence at all to justify this belief. Merriman may have been a small farmer, but he was in no sense a cottier: he was a man of modest but definite substance. Mac Gearailt probably lived in comfortable circumstances. There are several very definite suggestions of this in his poetry.

It is necessary to appreciate the economic and social structure of Cork, Waterford and Kerry in this period. In much of the countryside it revolved around dairy farming. The criterion of wealth in these regions was cattle. Seán Ó Murchadha (Ráithíneach) used the term 'fear míle bó' to indicate a rich man.[70] In his *Aithrí*, Donnchadh Ruadh Mac Conmara advised:

Ná cuirimís speóis i mbó ná i maoin
I gciste ná i stór ná i ngeoin an tsaoghail.[71]

References in the poetry to dowries often mention cattle explicitly.
In one poem, Eoghan Ruadh Ó Súilleabháin declaimed:

Rachmas ná spréidh ní ghlacfainn-se léi-se
airgead, tréad ná bán-stoc.[72]

Milch-cattle as part of a dowry enter again in *Caoineadh Airt Uí
Laoghaire:*

Is mó bean chumtha chórach
Ó Chorcaigh na seolta
Go Droichead na Tóime
Do thabharfadh macha mór bó dhuit.[73]

Máire Bhuidhe Ní Laoghaire's poems afford other examples. In
Fáinne an lae for instance, we read the sentiment:

Do phósfainn-se gan feoirling thú
Is ní iarrfainn ba ná spré.[74]

More explicit is the reference in *An Búrcach:*

Muna mbeadh crosa is fán an tsaoighil
Is bás a h-athar féin
Bheadh flúirse mhór dá stoc annsúd
I ngaorthadh cúmhra réidhe.[75]

Cattle were a yardstick of wealth. The smaller cattle owners sometimes looked after them themselves, but it was customary for cattle
owners, often small ones, to rent cattle and land to dairymen for a
rent often paid in part at least in kind. The occupation was poor and
mean even in popular esteem. Dinneen has quoted some verses in
defence of a member of the Burke family who had been referred to
slightingly because he was reduced to herding cattle:

Ní masladh ná tarcaisne dhon Bhúrcach
Bheith ag casadh ná ag múscailt a bhó
Mar dá athair ba chleachtach d'réir dúthchais
Fairsinige phunnach 'n-a gcomhair;
A eachra chapallaibh lúthmhar,

Ba mhinic é a gcúrsa i dtigh an óil,
An fhaid bhí an aicme seo a dubhairt é
Ar fuaid gharraidhthe is dronn ortha ag tóch.[76]

In describing the decline in the fortunes of 'An Búrcach', these lines also provide the contrast between two different social classes.

Art Ó Laoghaire was probably a prosperous cattle-owning tenant farmer: Eibhlín Dubh states in one line: Tá do bha bhuí á gcrú.[77] Art may well have marketed the butter from his dairymen tenants in Cork: the lines:

> bhíodh mná na gceannaithe
> Ag umhlú go talamh duit[78]

suggest this. Families such as this lived in considerable comfort. In the Lament or Caoineadh for her husband, Eibhlín Dubh declaimed:

> Chuiris parlús á ghealadh dhom
> Rúmanna á mbreacadh dhom,
> Bácús á dheargadh dhom . . .
> Rósta ar bhearaibh dhom
> Mairt á leagadh dhom.[79]

Or again consider the picture conjured up by the following lines describing how Arthur O'Leary entertained those who hunted with him:

> Á mbreith isteach don halla,
> Mar a mbíodh faobhar á chur ar sceanaibh,
> Muiceoil ar bord á gearradh,
> Caoireoil ná comhaireofaí a heasnaí,
> Coirce craorach ramhar
> A bhainfeadh sraoth as eachaibh—
> Capaill ghruagach' sheanga
> Is buachaillí 'na n-aice
> Ná bainfí díol ina leaba
> Ná as fásach a gcapall
> Dá bhfanaidís siúd seachtain.[80]

Piaras Mac Gearailt's lament for Máire Paor suggests a not dissimilar scene:

Id chistin ar crochadh bhíodh borradh-mhairt mhéithe;
Id phroinn-teach measaim dob' fhairsing do thréithe
Ag riaradh bídh agus dighe gach féile. . . .
Id halla do chínn-se gasradh gléigeal
Bláth do chuim-se, a ríogha aobhdha;
Fir agus mná dhuit gach lá ag géilleadh.[81]

Families such as these are scarcely representative. But at a more
modest level there is also evidence of comfort. In Máire Bhuidhe
Ní Laoghaire's *Caoineadh Sheáin de Búrca*, we read:

Gheobhainn plúr mín muilinn 'á rilleadh trí h-áirse
Rósta milis agus imirt ar tháiplis
Marcuíocht ar eachaibh groidhe stábla.[82]

Families owning cattle and living in circumstances which were very
comfortable by the standards of the age, considered themselves the
social equal of the Anglo-Irish families in their areas. In many ways
their economic circumstances were similar to those of the Anglo-
Irish families in the Mallow area to whom Eoghan Ruadh Ó
Súilleabháin referred contemptuously as 'lucht dreadair bhriste
meadrach do dhíol thar lear'.[83] Such Irish families preserved an
aristocratic sense of injustice and of a right to the lands now
owned by descendants of the original Cromwellian or Williamite
planters. Some of these tensions come through the lines of *Caoineadh
Airt Uí Laoghaire*, for instance:

D'umhlaídís Sasanaigh
Síos go talamh duit,
Is ní ar mhaithe leat
Ach le haon-chorp eagla.

. . .

Tar éis teacht duit thar sáile
Glantaí an tsráid duit
Is ní le grá dhuit
Ach le han-chuid gráine ort.[84]

In housing too they often lived in the new style of slated dwellings.
This style of dwelling—the new slated house—as well as mode of
living are suggested in the imagery of one of Eoghan Ruadh Ó
Súilleabháin's love poems where he promises:

22

Mar béidh againn mór-chuid de mhacha buaibh ann
Is eacha ruadha, mear, gléasta
Ar gcríocha cruachta le linn ár snuadhchair
Is slinn ar chúirt bhreágh aolbhaigh.[85]

In tone and outlook the Munster poetry appears that of well-to-do, comfortable families, either families on a social par with Anglo-Irish families or families of lesser social pretensions but still like those in Máire Bhuidhe Ní Laoghaire's circle living in modest but definite comfort. Even in the poetry of Donnchadh Ruadh Mac Conmara, something of this outlook emerges in the strength of his disavowal of manual labour:

Ní fhaicfar mo dhrom-sa ag cur allais go reamhar
Ag greafadh ná ag treabhadh éan-am den bhliain,
Gheobhad atharrach leabhair, béad im Shasanach teann
Os aca bhíonn togha agus rogha gach biadh.[86]

The Munster poetry is essentially aristocratic in outlook. It lacks the intimacy with local life that often emerges in Ulster or Connacht poetry. The case for this poetry representing a peasant outlook or for its being the poetry of peasants—to use Corkery's term—is weak. This does not necessarily disprove the case for a Hidden Ireland, but the Hidden Ireland revealed in it is almost certainly that of better-off families or of those bearing a strong aristocratic sense of identification. It throws little light on the outlook of ordinary peasants, and more positively very little at all on their working or living conditions. The great bulk of Munster peasants did not have enough resources to own cattle but rented them from a cattle-owning family. Richer cattle-owners such as Art Ó Laoghaire were in effect middlemen. A Catholic landowner has painted an unsympathetic picture of these families, speaking scornfully of the

pride, drunkenness and sloth of the middling sort among the Irish. Every one of them thinks himself too great for any industry except taking farms. When they happen to get them they screw enormous rents from some beggarly dairyman and spend their whole time in the alehouse of the next village. If they have sons they are all to be priests, physicians or French officers.[87]

This picture is unsympathetic; landlords did not take kindly to the independence and pride of outlook characteristic of such tenants. However, it is important to remember that the picture often painted of the way of life of middlemen would be applicable to some of the poets and more definitely to the way of life eulogised in their work. Arthur Young had spoken of 'your fellows with round hats, edged with gold, who hunt in the morning, get drunk in the evening and fight the next morning'.[88] Young's lines, for instance, sound almost like a paraphrase of the lines in Seán na Ráithíneach's *Spás le h-aer* and *Mo shlán-sa feasta*, in particular of the following lines in the latter poem:

> Dánta is damhas is báire ar faithche
> Agus námhaid do leagadh le righin-dair,
> Cáirt is dramanna ar chách do scaipeadh.[89]

Hunting figured prominently as well, as in *Spás le h-aer:*

> Spuir is fuip ó thigh go tigh
> Ag dul 's ag rith go malairt dighe
> Coin is groigh is cothrom suilth
> 'S i dtosach truip do chleachtaimís.[90]

The Munster poetry of the eighteenth century is very eulogistic of conviviality and gregarious drinking. Ravishing or kidnapping of heiresses are, as Lecky pointed out, not as common as was suggested by Froude. But whereas Corkery suggested that it was conducted by Protestant bucks, this was by no means the case. Professor Ó Tuama's careful account of Art Ó Laoghaire would appear to suggest that incidents of this nature entered into the background of Ó Laoghaire's quarrel with Morris, although it may have been his followers rather than himself who were responsible.[91]

Fighting or the ability to fight in what appear to be ancestral forms of the more familiar faction fight of the nineteenth century are often described approvingly in the poetry of the period. There are a few fleeting references in Eoghan Ruadh Ó Súilleabháin's poetry, and in Mac Conmara's, a single reference in Mac Craith's,[92] and some very positive ones in Seán na Ráithíneach Ó Murchadha's poetry. In one of her poems, giving matrimonial advice to a son, Máire Bhuidhe Ní Laoghaire advised him:

> A Bhúrcaigh Óig ó'n gCéim . . .
> Ná fág í siúd id dhéidh
> Mar gheall ar bheagán spré

Dá dtigheadh a clan sa bhruighin let ais
Go mbuadhfaoi leat an sway.[93]

Cattle-owning was of course very much a feature of the south-west even before the eighteenth century; it is reflected in the poetry. The difference between the earlier cattle owners and those of the eighteenth century is that the latter were tenant farmers. They were however quite comfortable varying from rich middlemen to more modest families with enough resources to provide dowries often in the form of cattle for their daughters. The pattern of life that revolved around dairying is conveyed in some of the lines in one of Eoghan Ruadh's poems:

Maidean fhuar fhliuch ag éighre suas dam,
Ag taisteal cuanta, is caolta,
'Seadh dhearcas mór-chuid do mhacha buaibh ann,
Is ainnir stuamdha dá n-aodharuigheacht;

. . .

'Sé mo dhaid adubhairt liom chomh moch so gluaiseacht,
Go raibh na ba 'san tuar ag géimrigh
Is gur thastuigh buachaill na mbó so ag buaint uaidh
Mar bhí an bhroid ró-chruaidh go léir air.[94]

Dairying in the early eighteenth century was fairly limited even in the south-west and prices unprofitable. But it subsequently grew rapidly as prices improved. Cattle-owning increased substantially, and it is hard to deny that profitability existed in the business. Things were very different for cottiers or for many of the dairymen who rented cattle. It is essential however to identify the comfortable section that existed and could expand, and wrong to assume as Corkery has done that their outlook and aspirations reflected those of the rural population as a whole. What Corkery has achieved is a dangerous confusion in which the living conditions and housing of the poorest are combined with the outlook and aspirations of the relatively prosperous among the native population.

What seems a striking indication of the restricted social class whose condition is reflected in the Munster poetry of the eighteenth century is the fact that there is scarcely any reference in that poetry to domestic employment in the textile industries.[95] One would not expect such reference in poetry of the late seventeenth or early eighteenth century, because at that time domestic weaving and spinning were not prevalent and in fact do not appear ever to have become widely diffused in some districts. But domestic industry in combing wool, or spinning and weaving both linen and wool spread very rapidly after the early decades of the century, especially in county Cork which developed textile activity, at once varied and extensive. Less deeply, the movement also affected county Kerry. Yet reference is almost totally lacking in south Munster poetry. As far as I am aware, the only references are in two poems by Eoghan Ruadh Ó Súilleabháin. In one of these, *Moladh Eanaigh*, there is a verse praising textile activity in the district in rather formal terms.[96] In the other, *A ghaibhne chláir Fódla, mo chomhairle anois déanaidh*, the items which the smith praised by the poet can make include the axle of the spinning wheel, cards for wool, hackles for linen, and wool combs.[97] These references are themselves totally lacking in the intimacy of the associations suggested frequently in Connacht and Ulster poetry. Piaras Mac Gearailt's poem, *An snaoisín*, does not refer to textile activity, although according to the later oral source for the poem, it was written about an occasion on which Mac Gearailt had to go into a farmer's house where six women were spinning.[98] Yet poetry such as Mac Gearailt's is silent on such industry. The likely reason is that the Munster poetry reflected the interests and conditions of the relatively well-to-do, whereas the poetry of Connacht and Ulster was at once less formal and less restricted to the interests and outlook of a relatively narrow class. Interestingly, Merriman's poem *Cúirt an Mheán-oíche*, from county Clare in 1780, refers to the textile industry, at that time growing rapidly in the county. The old man in describing the cabin which the girl came from, declaims:

Garbh ná mín, ní síntear fút ann
Barrach nó líon dar sníomhadh le túirne.[99]

In turn, in the course of what seems to be intended as a reply in kind, the girl claims that among the unfulfilled matrimonial promises of the old man were the provision of 'olann is líon le sníomh chun éadaigh'.[100] What is significant is that these references appear to imply an equation between spinning and comfort or security. Spinning or weaving were rarely resorted to by really well-off farming or cattle-owning farmers. They were more often the resort of cottiers and small farmers who could not hope to live out of the income of a small farm or agricultural employment. One might be prepared to regard the lines:

26

A rún mo chléibh, nach mar siúd ab fhearr duit
tús do shaoil a chaitheamh liom
is gan a bheith i gclúid faoi léan ag búr gan chéill
i gceann túirne is péire cárdaí

in Ó Doirnín's *Úrchnoc Chéin Mhic Cáinte* as a poetic image,[101]
except that references to employment in the linen industry crop up
elsewhere in his poetry. In *Sabha Nic Oireachtaigh*, for instance, the
lines:

> beidh mise ag ceannach snátha ar aontaí ó mhná
> agus línéadach bán glégeal.[102]

Or, in *Dá mbeinnse saidhbhir:*

> is duisín déanta ó mo mhnaoi go gléasta,
> sníofa óna méara go sleamhain slim.[103]

Such lines are a good deal more realistic than the rather stilted lines
by Eoghan Ruadh Ó Súilleabháin. More realistic still are the lines
by Uilliam Ó Maoil Chiaráin in *Ceol do chum Uilliam 'aol Chiaráin
tráth chuaidh a bhean Sighle go Cúig' Uladh a cheannacht barraigh:*

Is fada bhreathnaigh mé ós íseal go raibh Sighle dá
    mheabhradh
A' síor bhailiughadh gach pighinn bheag dá ndéanadh sí
    ar abhras.[104]

Weaving and spinning often enter into Galway and Mayo poetry,
starting perhaps with Riocard Bairéad's satirical *Eoghan Cóir* in 1788.

> Ba soirbh ag tógáil an chíos é,
> Is ba bheag aige mí nó dhó
> Nó go ndíoltái an bhó ar an aonach,
> Nó an giota bhí ins an tseol.[105]

Raftery's poems have many references. Such mention in the Connacht poetry is all the more impressive because so much of it
(Raftery's evidence, for instance) comes from a period when domestic
textile industry was declining rapidly.

The Munster poetry, it is argued here, reflects the outlook of a
far from insubstantial though still restricted class. The sense of

27

oppression that it has suggested to many should be attributed rightly to identification by this group with the landed class uprooted in the social and political upheavals of the seventeenth century. References to rents in this poetry have often been interpreted as illustrating the oppressive character of the land system of the eighteenth century. Mac Gearailt, for instance, wrote: 'Is cásmhar sinn gan spás fé chíos go cráite, claoite, ciúin, bocht'.[106] Mac Conmara saw the hills of Ireland:

> ag gallaphoic síos fé ghreim, mo léan
> 'S a mbailte dá ríomh fé chíos go daor.[107]

Eoghan Ruadh complained:
> Mo thréad
> Fá fhíor-smacht ag gallaibh gan cheannas gan réim
> Ag taxanna daora dá gcartadh gach bliadhain.[108]

These statements are largely rhetorical. They are on the same lines as and perhaps directly imitative of Seán Clárach's example:

> . . . na céadta
> Tá ag screadaigh 's ag béicigh
> Dá gcreachadh is dá gcéasadh le móirchíos.[109]

The tone of exaggeration seems evident, and was sometimes done humourously as when Mac Craith attributed his exile, due to personal reasons, to 'dlighthe cruadha na Whigs do ruaig mé in imeall Tuaithe im aonar'.[110] The poetry as a whole is remarkably non-specific in instancing oppression. Names are sometimes instanced as by Piaras Mac Gearailt's lines:

> Maud is Moor is Bagwell d'ár gcárnadh ins gach céim
> Fowkes is Hoop is Barrett, triúr d'fhúig mé-se i n-earáid.[111]

These are, however, alliterative devices directly imitating what Seán Clárach did in at least two poems.[112] Mac Craith [113] did the same, as did Eoghan Ruadh Ó Súilleabháin in a *A fhile chirt ghéir*, the most elaborate instance of this practice.[114] Seán Clárach's lines:

> Atá an tóir ar mo mhullach
> Go minic ó thighearna an stáit
> Atá mo bhróga-sa briste
> Is gan pinginn dá bhfiacha im láimh.[115]

28

are simply an exercise in rhetoric and exaggeration. A poem such as his *Colonel Dawson*, referring to a specific case of oppressive activity, seems to be altogether exceptional.[116] Seán na Ráithíneach Ó Murchadha's poetry is particularly interesting: he was not involved in the *aisling* genre apart from fleeting references to the downfall of the Gaelic aristocracy and their poetic supports. Vague general references to oppression under rent are absent from his poetry. In his elegiac poems there are references in very conventional terms to the praised parties' leniency with rents; there are also a few poems attacking bailiffs or middlemen who rack-rented. The picture his poetry would suggest is hardly one of an oppressive land system.

IV

Once the aristocratic nostalgia for the past waned, concern with rents in the poetry declined very markedly. In Raftery's poetry references to rent are almost invariably perfunctory; e.g. in *Cill Aodáin*: 'dheamhain caint ar pighinn cíosa ann ná dadaidh d'á shórt'[117]. Bairéad's *Eoghan Cóir* confines itself to satirising the bailiff;[118] the poem affords no ground for more general deduction. There is even by one of the Callanan brothers a poem warmly praising a bailiff.[119]

Not only is there very little evidence in the poetry to suggest that rents operated to make an oppressive land system, but the poetry appears to afford some definite evidence that, contrary to what the hidden-Ireland concept would suggest, poets did not see rents as a factor discouraging activity. Far from rent being the obsession, the practical concern was with prices. Uilliam Ó Maoil Chiaráin's concern in the first half of the eighteenth century had been simple: 'an t-earradh bheith daor go ndéanfamuis an cíos'.[120] A century later Marcas Ó Callanáin in county Galway declared:

> Is féadfaidh tú bheith ag ól seal
> Ó d'éirigh an t-arbhar daor.[121]

If Ó Maoil Chiaráin did not work harder, it was largely because he did not wish to exert himself, not because the incentive was lacking:

> Bíonn sise Sighle i gcorraidhe a choidhch' liom
> Mar nach ndéanaim dí gníomh ná fóghnamh;
> Mar nach gcuirim-se síol, coirce, nó líon di,

Meacainí buí nó pónar;
An measann sibh, a dhaoine, nach mise tá críonna
Nach mbriseann mo chroidhe le foghnamh
'S liacht óganach saoitheamhail a bheirfeadh *relief* damh
A' teacht na féil' Michil sa' bhfoghmhar.[122]

Far from the poetry suggesting survival at subsistence level, it suggests that a definite level of comfort could be enjoyed by the farmer. For Ó Maoil Chiaráin, this level consisted of:

Dá mbeirfinn-se beo 'gus sealbhán bó
A bheith agam, nó scór de chaoirigh,
Seisreach nó dhó de chaiple breagh óg,
A bheith agam ar nós an tsaothraigh.[123]

Ó Maoil Chiaráin clearly took as a matter of course that the small farmer could add to his capital or alternatively dissipate his resources in drink, as he chose. In *Ceol póiteóireachta* he wrote:

Bíonn dream ann a shanntuigheas maoin airgid agus ór,
Dream eile a shanntuigheas maoin chaorach agus bó;
Dar liomsa b'fhearr roinn do gach cuid aca ól
Ná an t-iomlán a bheith caillte tráth theighid faoi'n bhfód.[124]

The same concept—that the farmer could with care enlarge his wealth—emerges in Ó Doirnín's *Sábha Nic Oireachtaigh*— itself an interesting poem as it suggests the various ways in which money was acquired in a farming community:

Tréigfidh mé ceol, cuideachta is spórt
agus cromfaidh mé le fónamh chun an tsaoil seo,
ceannóchaidh mé bó, capall nó dhó
agus, b'fhéidir, gabhair agus caoirigh.[125]

The picture of modest comfort and competence emerges in Raftery's *Caismirt an phótaire leis an uisge-beatha*:

Is deas an rud bólacht, féar maith agus gabháltas
Cruithneacht agus eórna le gearradh
Min in san gcófra, gus teine tráthnóna
Agus dídean d'fhear bóthair a's bealaigh,
Léine 'gus cóta ag an Aifrionn Dia Domhnaigh,
Hata 'gus cóta 'san bhfaisiún.[126]

Marcus Ó Callanáin's picture in *An Lái* is remarkably similar in content:

B'fhearr an capall dom, cliath agus céachta,
Seisreach capall gabhtha gléasta,
Chuirfeadh na bánta ar chúl a chéile.

Is ina n-aice ba mhinic sin bólacht,
Tine agus teas ag fear bealaigh agus bóthair,
Beatha go fairsing, airgead agus ór buí,
Éadach sa bhfaisean ag daoine críona agus óga.[127]

We have come to regard early and romantic marriage as a feature of pre-Famine Ireland. Late marriage and the mercenary considerations revolving around the made match are considered as features emerging in post-Famine Ireland. If however the pre-Famine Irishman was often a man of modest substance, and not as has been stated a man of cottier or cottier-like condition, the economic basis for the made match and the dowry already existed. The dowry was always significant in cattle-owning families in Munster. But reference to the dowry is by no means confined to the Munster poetry. The word match and its economic connotations was already well-established before the Great Famine. In one of his poems, *A Sheáin a mhic mo chomharsan* Marcas Ó Callanáin wrote of a locality:

Má tá tú ag dul ag pósadh . . .
Téirigh go Suí Finn;
Tá airgead is ór ann,
Agus meaitseannaí go leor ann.[128]

In a much earlier poem, from Ulster, by Father Pól Ó Briain, we have a clear expression of the popular attitudes which applied to the dowry system:

A Phóil mhic Bhriain má phós tusa an chailleach,
Gan airgead, gan earradh, gan chaoirigh, gan bhuaibh,
'Sé bhreathnuighim in mo chéill go raibh tú ar mearadh,
Tráth b'fhéidir do mhealladh le mnaoi gan duais.[129]

The word *spré* or dowry is mentioned time and time again in the poetry from every province especially with the romantic compliment that the poet would willingly marry the girl without a dowry. The

Ulster poet Pádraig Ó Briain in *Moladh Hanna Ní Chrosáin* wrote:

> Dá bhfuighfinn-se Hanna cha n-iarrfainn spré léith,
> Agus thuillfinn féin a gcaithfeadh sinn.[130]

Seán Ó Murchadha expressed the identical sentiment in *Do seoladh mé ar bainis:*

> A pósadh pé ghealladh ba mhargadh saor
> Gan spré ar bith i gcunntus a faghála.[131]

A still more emphatic declaration by Seán Ó Murchadha about a young lady was:

> Is dearbh gurbh fhearra d'fhear is í taobhnocht
> 'ná falcaire seasc gan mhaith is trí spré aici.[132]

Eoghan Ruadh Ó Súilleabháin declared the disinterest of his love by proclaiming:

> Is pé méad a spré ní ghlaodhfainn choidhche a leath.[133]

The theme comes up in Raftery's poetry from time to time as well. In *Bríd Bhéasaigh:*

> 'S ní iarrfainn leat mar fhéirín
> Acht mé a's tú bheith i n'éinfheacht.[134]

The universality of this theme in the love poems of the eighteenth and early nineteenth century would only make sense if the dowry system was equally universal.[135] Dowries themselves underline the fact that a substantial proportion of the rural population enjoyed some substance. On what dowries amounted to in exact terms, poetry, as one would expect, hardly throws light. But fifty sovereigns 'besides many articles which she has in store' is mentioned in one poem by **Marcus** Ó Callanáin.[136] Dowries were of course often in kind, as the poetry suggests, especially in districts where animal husbandry was well established. In dairying districts, dowries for marriages arranged between families of small and large farmers took the form of a transfer of milch cattle.

We must, I think, conclude that the hidden Ireland, taking its existence for granted for the moment, was not marked by the prevalence or degree of poverty suggested by Corkery. If we take a single aspect, diet, for instance, we can see a much more varied pattern than that gleaned from a reading of Corkery's pages. Uilliam Ó Maoil Chiaráin's *Slán d'fhearaibh Laighean* is a nostalgic contrast between the parts of Meath where he had lived and the poorer conditions in Machaire Cluain in county Monaghan. Some lines of the poems convey a vivid sense of farming life and standards in county Meath:

Ní fheicim, ná na caoirigh a' méilthigh ar na
    machairibh bán,
Eachraidh dhá dtréineáil i ndiaidh gadhar 'dol
    trasna na bhfál,
        . . .

Meacainí ná rútaí ná nuaidheacht ar bith 'teacht i
    láthair;
Acht ag teacht mí na Lughnasa crúsach a bhainfidhe
    le spáid.

Chan fheicim an fheoil 'na spólaibh ins na stallaibh
    dhá díol,
Chan fheicim an eorna 'na scóraibh ná an
    chruinneachta mhaol,
Gas pise nó pónair mar nach dúthchas dóibh a theacht
    in bhur dtír.
        . . .

Chan fheicim na stácaí gan bheárnadh in bhur
    n-agart fá Fhéil' Eóin,
Chan fheicim, ná na pátruin mar 'a ghnáthach
    a bheith againn ag Bóinn.[137]

Meat on sale in stalls at fairs or markets would suggest a prosperous area. Around 1820-1830 a poem by Peadar Mac Ualgairg of an insensitive and satirical nature about a *spailpín* has the following lines implying the dietary contrast:

Muna beith go bhfuil mé ramhar téagarta le hithe
    na feola
Shiubhailfinn-se leat tamall go gcuirfinn thú ar an
    eolas.[138]

Even a century previously, the haymaking and harvesting seasons in Meath had seasonally attracted labour from the poorer districts in Ulster. A poem by Art Mac Cubhthaigh, *Nansaidh Ní Dhuilleachain*, is the sole evidence of the seasonal migration of labour in that region in that period—a rather striking testimony of the value which literary material, cautiously used, can have for the historian. Nansaidh Ní Dhuilleachain was a maid in a bar at Tallonstown on the migrants' route back from their work in Meath:

> Na hUltaigh a bhíos tuirseach gan bhrígh
> Ag filleadh ón Mhidhe go tréith-lag,
> Théid go bruidhin Uí Dhuilleachain 'san oidhche
>
> . . .
>
> Cluinim-se go luath ag an mhacraidh teacht anuas.
> Pilleadh ó n-a gcuairt fhoghmhair.[139]

Migrant labourers came from poorer districts, and lived on a poorer diet. We have here a reminder of the social complexity of the scene which tends to be engulfed in Corkery's account by the concept of a few big houses in a universal sea of poverty. A diet confined to potatoes was by no means socially universal. The line 'Ba sógh leis prátaí is dríodar bláthaighe d'fhagháil' in Eoghan Ruadh Ó Súilleabháin's *Barántas do Dhomhnall Ó Dálaigh* as a vehicle of ridicule seems to suggest that such a diet was regarded by the poet with some degree of contempt.[140] All but the very poor had a fairly varied diet. In fairly comfortable farming families, bread was quite common. In Máire Bhuidhe Ní Laoghaire's poem *An Búrcach*, there is reference to a woman who

> Thuill clú agus meas riamh d'fhagháil;
> Seomraí brúchtaigh bhán
> Is machaí bó ag tál
> Mná deaghchlúmhail 'na dtithe siúd
> Do riarfadh flúirse aráin.[141]

But this bread was almost certainly oatmeal or barley bread even for a social milieu with a certain economic competence such as hers. This is suggested by the fact that in her poem about the expected French landing wheat is mentioned as one of the items they would have on their own table if the French landed and rents were eliminated.[142]

Almost paradoxically, as Corkery's account of the Hidden Ireland is so filled with poverty, it does not deal with the poor at all. Numerous they were too, and their poverty by our modern European standards deep. Moreover, there is reason to believe that living conditions of the lower classes deteriorated at an earlier date and more sharply in Munster than in the other provinces. The Munster poetry does not document their condition at all. What is striking, however, about economic life as it emerges through the poetry of all the provinces is the extent to which money circulated. To some extent, this is of course only a reflection of the fact that very often the poetry reflected standards which were above the lowest level in the rural community. But whether this is the case or not, it is an added reason why one must be cautious about accepting a sharp distinction between a subsistence and a cash or maritime economy. Indeed, in a relatively poor community, not only was money essential as in all communities, but because there was a pressing demand for cash it was sometimes necessary to pay in advance. Eoghan Ruadh, as *Easmailt is ár* suggests, had paid his four pence in advance for the mending of his pair of stockings.[143] One of Raftery's poems reveals that the shoe-maker might be paid in advance as well.[144]

In an age preceding that of the factory or imported article, local specialization was general enough to make the use of money essential for all, despite regional self-sufficiency. Poems in praise of smiths and carpenters testify not only to their number but to their importance. Raftery's *Cnocán an Eanaigh* is a reminder about the variety of occupations that existed (in fact until late in the nineteenth century) in rural areas:

> Níl figheadóir nó haitéaraidhe, gréasaidhe, táilliúr,
> Ó abhainn Loch Carn go Baile Loch' Riach
> Nó fear déanta táirne, gabh' dubh, nó ceárdaidhe
> Nó fear maide-rámh nach dtógfadh sé a chroidhe.[145]

Some of these craftsmen were active enough to have employees working for them. Of Seán Ó Bránáin, Raftery declared:

> Buachaillí, lán sráide
> A bhíos ag ithe 's ag codladh 'ge,
> Seán a bheireas obair dhóibh
> Agus páigh mhaith d'á réir.[146]

Employment for a money wage was a familiar concept. Eoghan Ruadh Ó Súilleabháin in *A chara mo chléibh* quotes the wages of a day labourer in Galway:

Ní stadfad go dtéad im réim don Ghaillimh lem ráin,
Mar a ngeobhad gach lae mo raol is breacfast mar phágh.[147]

Pádraig Ó Briain of Grangegeeth in putting the following words of
reproof of his idle ways in the mouth of his wife, throws some light
on the alternatives at the bottom of the social scale:

Nach mb'fhearr damhsa oibridhe a d'imtheóchadh
    na sglábhaidhe,
Agus bheirfeadh dhamh a pháidhe i ndeireadh gach lae,
Nó stócach bacaigh a d'iompróchadh a mhála,
Agus roinnfeadh le mo pháistibh a gcruinneóchadh
    sé de dhéirc,
Ná do léithid . . ..[148]

V

The Hidden-Ireland concept emerges through Corkery's book as a
very unsatisfactory one. It misreads the outlook expressed in the
poetry, reads into the poetry aspirations which it did not contain,
and thus creates a continuity from aristocratic resentment to
popular unrest more artificial than real. The outlook is presented
against a background of economic and social oppression, although
the background like the outlook rests largely on the same evidence
and on the handling or interpretation of it. The mistake of interpretation is cumulative. The interpretation of the poetry and the background to the poetry was also powerfully influenced by the national
and cultural renaissance at the end of the nineteenth century and the
beginning of the twentieth. Dinneen, Hyde and the other editors of
the poetic material of the seventeenth and eighteenth centuries were
children of their era; its preoccupations influenced their interpretation of the character of the poetry and the ideas expressed in it, and
enhanced—in fact created—a deceptive element of continuity.
Corkery read little history, came to the language and literature late
in life, and lacked original historical insights of his own. He developed
systematically a concept which already existed less explicitly in the
writings of others, Dinneen in particular.

A Hidden Ireland may well exist; by definition a Hidden Ireland,
or for that matter several hidden Irelands—if we compartmentalise
studies—must exist in the sense that there are aspects or dimensions

to what happened in human activity and experience that escape the prying eye of the historian. Literary evidence is relevant to their study, because it can throw light on attitudes poorly or imperfectly reflected in the more formal documents on which historians as a rule rely. Corkery's concept of a Hidden Ireland rests, however, on a misreading of certain significant features of the poetry of the period, and on certain assumptions flowing in part from his reading of the poetry, in part from the character of the national revival of the early twentieth century. His Hidden Ireland simplifes Irish history, putting it in a simple context of land resettlement, oppression and resentment with predictable and stereotyped relationships and situations flowing from it. It also seems to impoverish Irish nationality and the sense of identity, seeing it in the context of settlement and oppression, and not in the rich, complex and varied stream of identity and racial consciousness heightened in the course of centuries of Anglo-Irish relations.

NOTES
With translations by Máirín Ní Dhonnchadha

1. D. Corkery, *The Hidden Ireland* (4th impression, Dublin 1956) vii. Subsequent references in the text of this essay refer to this work.
2. K. H. Connell, 'Catholicism and marriage in the century after the Famine' in *Irish Peasant Society* (Oxford 1968).
3. P. Ua Duinnín, *Muinntir Chiarraidhe roimh an droch-shaoghal* (Dublin 1905) 1: 'in speaking of the people of Kerry, I speak of the people of all Munster'.
4. J. A. Froude, 'A fortnight in Kerry', 2 parts, in *Short studies on great subjects* ii (London 1894); *The two chiefs of Dunboy* (London 1889).
6. See especially J. A. Froude, 'A fortnight in Kerry', 'Ireland since the Union', *Short studies on great subjects* ii (London 1894); 'On the uses of a landed gentry', *op. cit.* iii (London 1893).
7. J. A. Froude, 'Ireland since the Union', *Short studies . . .* ii 523.
8. J. A. Froude, 'A fortnight in Kerry', *op. cit.* ii 261.
9. J. A. Froude, 'On the uses of a landed gentry', *op. cit.* iii 407.
10. J. A. Froude, 'A fortnight in Kerry, *op. cit.* ii 217.
11. J. A. Froude, 'Ireland since the Union', *op. cit.* ii 520.
12. J. A. Froude, 'A fortnight in Kerry', *op. cit.* ii 272.
13. J. A. Froude, 'Ireland since the Union', *op. cit.* ii 553.
14. J. A. Froude, 'A fortnight in Kerry', *op. cit.* ii 305.
15. J. A. Froude, 'Ireland since the Union', *op. cit.* ii 545.
16. Paper read to the Irish Conference of Historians, University College, Dublin, May 1969.
17. See L. M. Cullen, 'The re-interpretation of Irish economic history', *Topic* 13 (Washington and Jefferson College, Washington, Penn.), Spring 1967, p. 69; 'Irish economic history: fact and myth' in *The formation of the Irish economy*: ed. L. M. Cullen (Cork 1969) 119-120.
18. D. Hyde (An Craoibhin Aoibhinn), *Abhráin atá leagtha ar an Reachtúire* (Dublin 1903). 14: 'and since we know that this blind man was an authority in the country, encouraging the people to oppose the tithes and inciting them against their enemies, his songs, be they good or bad, are worth collecting for that reason alone'.
19. P. Ua Duinnín, *Filidhe na Máighe* (Dublin 1906) xvi.
20. P. Ua Duinnín, *Amhráin Eoghain Ruaidh Uí Shuilleabháin*, 2nd ed. (Dublin 1902) xxvi. This view was first expressed in P. Ua Duinnín, *Dánta Aodhagáin Uí Rathaile* (London 1900) xxxvii.
21. P. Ua Duinnín, *Amhráin Sheaghain Chláraigh Mhic Dhomhnaill* (Dublin 1902) vi.
22. Editions of Feriter, Séafradh Ó Donnchadha, Ó Rathaile, Seán Clárach Mac Domhnaill, Eoghan Ruadh Ó Súilleabháin, Tadhg Gaedhealach Ó Súilleabháin and the Maigue poets.
23. P. Ua Duinnín, *Filidhe na Máighe* xvii.
24. P. Ua Duinnín, *Amhráin Eoghain Ruaidh Uí Shuilleabháin* (Dublin 1902) 2nd ed. p. xxxvii. 'Had he lived in a more favoured age he would assuredly have become the most brilliant writer of his time and shed lasting lustre on his country' (p. xii).
25. P. Ua Duinnín, *Filidhe na Máighe* xliv.
26. *Mo mhíle truagh, mo bhuaidhirt, mo bhrón* in Ua Duinnín, *Filidhe na Máighe* (Dublin 1906) 1: 'the Gaelic nobility in acute oppression'.

27. *Ba riaghail ag flaithibh* in R. Ó Foghludha, *Amhráin Phiarais Mhic Ghearailt* (Dublin 1905) 26: 'my sorrow and woe! the nobles wandering in subjection'.
28. R. Ó Foghludha, *Eoghan Ruadh Ó Súilleabháin* (Dublin 1937) 66: 'Cashel's lineage in dire bondage, paying heavy rent to English-speaking foreigners who took possession of the limed dwellings and the land of everyone I have recounted.'
29. *Comhchruinniú na Raghailleach* in É. Ó Muirgheasa, *Amhráin na Midhe* i (Dublin 1933) 42: 'but foreigners hold sway, since the O'Reillys and the O'Neills departed from us'.
30. É. Ó Muirgheasa, *Amhráin Airt Mhic Chubhthaigh agus Amhráin eile* i (Dundalk 1926) 39: 'Our leases and our pleasure subject to arrogant people.' The line of the text, 'Ma tíortha ag osnaigh faoi léan ar léagsaí', is a misquotation. The full citation is:
    A chéile na daonnacht' is féile dár shíolruigh,
    Nach léar duit na tíortha ag osnaigh faoi léan,
    Ar léagsaí 's ar n-aoibhneas ag géilleadh do chlainn díomuis,
    Is gur Papist is mian leo a ghoirm dár gcléir.
    This might be translated as –
    'Friend of humanity, most generous ever born,
    Do you not see the lands sighing in affliction,
    Our leases and our pleasure subject to arrogant people,
    And 'Papist' is what they wish to call our clergy.'
31. S. de Rís, *Peadar Ó Doirnín* (Dublin 1969) 31: 'There is no poor person dependent on a couple of cattle to whom I will not give a heifer and grazing, until the time when they will maintain stock and great wealth on hill-land and secure fixed terms and leases.'
32. R. Ó Foghludha, *Eoghan Ruadh Ó Súilleabháin* 76: 'for the Gaelic race will reign supreme in their own lands without a title in rent'.
33. É. Ó Muirgheasa, *Amhráin Airt Mhic Chubhthaigh agus Amhráin eile* i 36: 'And Séamus in lineage is a fresh branch of the same fair wood, of the ancestry of those people to whom estates and lands would pay ready obeisance in rent without any resentment.'
34. S. Ní Chinnéide, 'Dialann Uí Chonchúir', *Galvia* vi (1957) 6.
35. S. de Rís, *Peadar Ó Doirnín* xxxiii.
36. R. Ó Foghludha, *Amhráin Phiarais Mac Ghearailt* 17: 'the one who composed this poem has many empty speeches in his head, and may God help him in his lack of sense'.
37. *Op. cit.* 94: 'may God give sense to that demi-earl who uttered this poem, the one in question being Liam Inglis'.
38. R. Ó Foghludha, *Eoghan Ruadh Ó Súilleabháin* 53: 'I myself fear, o shining beauty, that this story you devised is a recitation of lies.'
39. *Op. cit.* 56.
40. T. O Raithbheartaigh, *Maighistrí san Fhilidheacht* (Dublin 1932) 171: 'that the poet was engaged in fantasy rather than feeling', and 173: 'I do not think that there is any nationalism in them'.
41. S. Ó Tuama, 'Dónal Ó Corcora agus filíocht na Gaeilge', *Studia Hibernica* 5 (1965) 33: 'What other king in eighteenth-century Ireland could better arouse the hope of salvation in the mind of the people.'
42. R. Ó Foghludha, *Eoghan Ruadh Ó Súilleabháin* 54: 'recount my tidings to the poets at home'.
43. D. Ó Donnchú, *Filíocht Mháire Bhuidhe Ní Laoghaire* (Dublin 1950) 39: 'Land will be without rent or payment, without levy or disputation, we will have wheaten flour and butter and fat meat on our own table.'

44. D. de hÍde (An Craoibhín Aobhinn), *Abhráin agus dánta an Reachtabhraigh* (Dublin 1933) 90. De hÍde indicates doubt about attributing it to Raftery. Its tone and language seem out of character with Raftery. It is probably earlier and by a different poet.' This game is of no consequence until the Spaniard comes and the king will lose his authority over Parliament, this is a departure which we will relish – the fair land will be ours for little rent. At the beginning of the season we will deal out slaughter, we will kill two thousand and one hundred cows, England's milking-places will have little lowing, at the beginning of the season, if we are still living. The poor man's cobblers will have plenty of leather, and we'll not ask a pair of them for less than a crown, we will have shoes without God awarding them and not eat a meal without meat any more.'

45. É. Ó Muirgheasa, *Amhráin Airt Mhic Chubhthaigh agus amhráin eile* ii 6-7. Ó Muirgheasa notes the attribution to Mac Cubhthaigh as 'open to some doubt' (*op. cit.* ii 50). In fact its outlook and sentiment seems totally out of character with Mac Cubhthaigh. 'They perjured themselves, I am no thief, despite my being frivolous, wayward and foolish, and were I to snatch the price of clothing from English-speaking louts, who would grudge it to Cathal Mhac Aoidh'; 'Deftly and bravely I would track down all his cows, no matter how dark the night.'

45a. Two sentences quoted in body of text without references translate as follows: 'The fair land will be ours for little rent' and 'Land will be without rent or payment, without levy or disputation.'

46. *Marbhna Airt Óig Uí Néill* in É. Ó Muirbheasa, *Amhráin Airt Mhic Chubhthaigh agus amhráin eile* i 20.

47. See e.g. the instances referred to by Corkery in his essay 'Filidheacht na Gaedhilge – a cineál' in R. Ó Foghludha, *Éigse na Máighe* (Dublin 1952) 21, and the poems relating to the conversion and entry into the ministry of the Dominican brother Donnchadh Ó hÉadromáin, *op. cit.* 80-84.

48. D. de hÍde (An Craoibhín Aoibhinn), *Abhráin agus dánta an Reachtabhraigh*. This is a more complete collection than his *Abhráin atá leagtha ar an Reachtúire* (Dublin 1903).

49. S. Ó Muireadhaigh, 'Na Fir Ribín', *Galvia* x (1964-65).

50. D. Ó Donnchú, *Filíocht Mháire Bhuidhe Ní Laoghaire* (Dublin 1950) 57: 'what every authority assures me in this book of Pastorini's is that before they finish the harvesting, they will make recompense for the excess'.

51. *Op. cit.* 64: 'What I heard from seers is that St John said to us that the respite they had has been exhausted, and that slaughter would come to every big-bottomed block who rejected Christ's Passion and enjoyed the excess.'

52. D. de hÍde (An Craoibhín Aoibhinn), *Abhráin agus dánta an Reachtabhraigh* 58: 'Pastorini wrote that it would come to pass that they would hold a meeting in every town, one day each month, in Clonmel there will be expulsion of New Lights and Orangemen, and it is in Loughrea that their destiny was proclaimed.'

53. *Op. cit.* 125: 'Pastorini wrote that we are not far from the day when foreigners will be overpowered and laid low, without anyone to keen them . . . but since Henry began his tricks, the Catholics are prostrate, but they will be ascendant again; they are nearing the time when Orangemen will be dispersed and informers cast out.'

54. *Op. cit.* 146: 'and that St John says in the revelation that the Gaels' exaction will be in the twenty-ninth year.'

55. É. Ó Muirgheasa, *Amhráin Airt Mhic Chubhthaigh agus amhráin eile* i 45-46.

56. In S. de Rís, *Peadar Ó Doirnín* 39-42. See also *Dá mbeinnse saibhir*, *op. cit.* 42-43.

41

57. E.g. the line *nuair a chaillfidh an sagart an tsainnt*, 'when the priest will lose his greed', quoted on page xxxii of Dineen's introduction to *Amhráin Eoghain Ruaidh Uí Shúilleabháin* 2nd ed. See also the poem *Os follas don chléir, op. cit.* 65-66.

58. 'The support of the Catholic clergy in Ireland 1750-1850' in J. L. McCracken (ed.), *Historical Studies* v (London 1965) 105, 114-117.

59. 'The Gaelic background' in M. Tierney (ed.), *Daniel O'Connell: nine centenary essays* (Dublin 1949).

60. J. H. Elliot, 'Revolution and continuity in early modern Europe', *Past and Present*, no. 42 (February 1969) 44.

61. S. Ó Tuama, *An grá in amhráin na ndaoine* (Dublin 1960) 290.

62. A. Young, *Tour in Ireland* (London 1780) 185.

63. P. Mac Cana, 'Irish literary tradition' in *A View of the Irish Language* (Dublin 1969) 45.

64. A. Young, *op. cit.* 249.

65. B. Ó Buachalla, *Peadar Ó Doirnín: amhráin* (Dublin 1969) 18: 'Such was the impoverishment of life that one might think it strange that any kind of poetry should develop.'

66. J. H. Elliot, *op. cit.* 48.

67. County Record Office, The Castle, Carlisle. Sir James Lowther, London, Oct. 8 1745 (No. 49).

68. Public Record Office, State Papers, Spain, S.P. 94/228. Joseph Jordan, letters at various dates in 1755.

69. S. Ó Tuama, *Caoineadh Airt Uí Laoghaire* (Dublin 1963) 9: 'It is not often that gentility or comfort is associated with Gaelic life in the eighteenth century. Nonetheless, it is true that there were households still living in relative ease here and there.'

70. Torna, *Seán na Ráithíneach* (Dublin 1954) 350: 'a man of a thousand cows'.

71. R. Ó Foghludha, *Donnchadh Ruadh Mac Conmara* (Dublin 1933) 64: 'Let us have no regard for cattle or wealth, for treasure or goods or the world's din.'

72. R. Ó Foghludha, *Eoghan Ruadh Ó Súilleabháin* 126: 'Neither wealth nor dowry would I accept with her, neither money, herd nor grazing stock.' (The word 'again' in the line of text following n. 72 should be removed – or some similar change be made – as the reference in this note is not definitely to 'milch-cattle'; *bán* in *bán-stoc* conotes either adjectival 'Áine, fair' etc., or – more likely – *bawn*, a field of grass which might be grazed by cattle – or stock – of any kind.)

73. S. Ó Tuama, *Caoineadh Airt Uí Laighaire* 36: 'Many is the handsome, well-built woman, from Cork of the sails to Toom Bridge, who would give you a herd of cows.'

74. D. Ó Donnchú, *Filíocht Mháire Bhuidhe Ní Laoghaire* 42: 'Without a farthing I would marry you, and not look for either cows or dowry.'

75. *Op. cit.* 49: 'Were it not for the afflictions and adversity of this world, and the death of her own father, a great store of her stock would be here in fragrant, level, river-grazing.'

76. P. Ua Duinnín, *Filidhe na Máighe*, p. xxvii: 'It is no reproach or insult to Burke to be driving or urging his cows, for his father was accustomed by inheritance to extensive lands in sheaves for them, his team of sinewy horses made their way frequently to the drinking-house, while the gang who said it were among the fields with bent backs from grubbing.'

77. S. Ó Tuama, *Caoineadh Airt Uí Laoghaire* 45: 'Your tawny cows are being milked.'

78. *Op. cit.* 43: 'The merchants' wives used to bow down to the ground before you.'

79. *Op. cit.* 33: 'You had a parlour bleached white for me, rooms decorated for me, bake-house made red for me, roasting on spits for me, beeves slaughtered for me.'
80. *Op. cit.* 42: 'Leading them into the hall, where knives used to be sharpened, pork at table carved, mutton with too many ribs for counting, oats red-ripe and plump which would make horses neigh – long-maned, slender horses and servant-lads beside them, for whose bed there would be no charge, nor for their horses' grazing, were they to stay a week.' See also p. 36, lines 88-90.
81. R. Ó Foghludha, *Amhráin Phiarais Mhic Ghearailt* 59: 'Hanging in your kitchen there used to be fleshy, fatted beeves; in your banqueting-hall your manner was bountiful – distributing food and drink at every feast . . . in your hall I used to see a comely band of youths, flower of your side, o beautiful queen, men and women paying homage to you each day.'
82. D. Ó Donnchú, *Filíocht Mháire Bhuidhe Ní Laoghaire* 52: 'I would get fine mill-flour, winnowed through arches, a tasty roast and playing at *táiplis*, riding on sturdy stable-horses.'
83. R. Ó Foghludha, *Eoghan Ruadh Ó Súilleabháin* 13: 'those who sell the inferior products of churns abroad'.
84. S. Ó Tuama, *Caoineadh Airt Uí Laoghaire* 34: 'The English used to bow down before you, and it was not to favour you but from sheer terror of you . . . . After your return from overseas, the street would be cleared before you, and it was not because of love for you but because of great aversion to you.'
85. P. Ua Duinnín, *Amhráin Eoghain Ruaidh Uí Shúilleabháin* 102: 'For we will have numerous herds of cows and swift, harnessed, bay horses, our lands in ricks when we have a family, and a slated roof on a fine lime-white mansion.'
86. R. Ó Foghludha, *Donnchadh Ruadh Mac Conmara* 57: 'My back will not be seen to sweat profusely in hoeing and ploughing at any time of the year, I will find a change of circumstances and be a well-to-do Englishman, for it is they who have the choicest and finest of fare.'
87. E. McLysaght (ed), *The Kenmare Papers* (Irish Manuscript Commission, Dublin 1942) 230.
88. A Young, *op. cit.* ii 79.
89. Torna, *Seán na Ráithíneach* 223-224. These lines are attributed to Seán Condún: 'Poems and dancing and a hurling-match on the field, enemies being laid low with stout oak, the distributing of quarts and drams to all.'
90. *Op. cit.* 226: 'With spurs and whip, running and racing, from one house to the next for diversity of drinking, hounds and horses and similar amusement, at the head of the troop used to be our wont.'
91. S. Ó Tuama, *Caoineadh Airt Uí Laighaire* 14-16.
92. A charaid chlúmhail dhíoghrais in R. Ó Foghludha, *Éigse na Máighe* 194-6: 195, *Gach dailc go pras nach cuibhe liom le righin-dair a chorp do chneadhainn*, 'every clod whom I dislike, with speed I used to lacerate with sturdy oak'.
93. D. Ó Donnchú, *Filíocht Mháire Bhuidhe Ní Laoghaire* 49: 'Young Burke from Kiskeam . . . do not leave her after you because of modest dowry, were her family to join you in the fray, the day would be carried by you.'
94. Ua Duinnín, *Amhráin Eoghain Ruaidh Uí Shúilleabháin* 100: 'When I arose one cold, wet morning, traversing harbours and marshy streams, I beheld in a place many herds of cows and a prudent maiden tending them . . . . It was my dad who told me to go forth this early, for the cows were lowing in the paddock-field, and he needed their herd for the grazing, for he was very hard-pressed in the task.'
95. There is of course occasional reference in seventeenth-century poetry to

43

ladies' skill in sewing and embroidery. This conventional praise is sometimes repeated in eighteenth-century poetry, e.g. Seán na Ráithíneach (Torna, *op. cit.* 120) and Eoghan Ruadh Ó Súilleabháin (R. Ó Foghludha, 94-96).

96. R. Ó Foghludha, *Eoghan Ruadh Ó Súilleabháin* 94-96.
97. P. Ua Duinnín, *Amhráin Eoghain Ruaidh Uí Shúilleabháin* 55-57.
98. R. Ó Foghludha, *Amhráin Phiarais Mhic Ghearailt* 92.
99. D. Ó hUaithne, *Cúirt an Mheán-oíche* (Dublin 1968) lines 405-406: 'Nothing is spread under you in it, be it rough or smooth, neither tow nor linen spun on the wheel.'
100. *Op. cit.* line 674: 'wool and linen for spinning as cloth'.
101. S. de Rís, *Peadar Ó Doirnín* 15: 'My own beloved, is that not how you would best spend your early years with me, rather than being miserable in a corner, crying senselessly and working a spinning-wheel and a pair of carders.'
102. *Op. cit.* 30: 'I will be buying thread from women at markets and white, clear-bright linen.'
103. *Op. cit.* 43: 'and a finished hank, in order, from my wife, spun smoothly and evenly by her fingers'.
104. É. Ó Muirgheasa, *Amhráin na Midhe* 23. (A song that Uilliam 'aol Chiaráin composed one time that his wife Sighle went to Ulster to buy tow): 'I have long observed secretly that Sighle was planning it, always collecting every few pennies which she used to make on handiwork.'
105. M. Ó Tiomanaidhe, *Abhráin Ghaedhilge an iarthair* (Dublin 1906): 'Affable he was in collecting the rent, and thought little of a month or two, until the cow would be sold at the market or the length which was on the loom.'
106. R. Ó Foghludha, *Amhráin Phiarais Mhic Ghearailt* 57: 'Sorry is our plight with no respite from rent, anguished, oppressed, subdued and poor.'
107. R. Ó Foghludha, *Donnchadh Ruadh Mac Conmara* 32: 'alas! in the crushing grip of foreign bucks, and their towns being reckoned in dire rents'.
108. R. Ó Foghludha, *Eoghan Ruadh Ó Súilleabháin* 77: 'My flock without authority or power, in true subjection to foreigners, harried by heavy taxes every year.'
109. R. Ó Foghludha, *Seán Clárach* 116: ' . . . hundreds who are screaming and crying out, being despoiled and tormented by great rent'.
110. R. Ó Foghludha, *Éigse na Máighe* 193: 'oppressive laws of the Whigs which banished me to the border of Tuath as a solitary'.
111. R. Ó Foghludha, *Amhráin Phiarais Mhic Ghearailt* 29: 'Maud and Moore and Bagwell ousting us at every step, Fowkes and Hoop and Bassett, three who left me vagrant.'
112. R. Ó Foghludha, *Seán Clárach* 106-107. The poems are *Is fada dham in uaigneas* and *Tá iarla chloinne Carrtha*.
113. R. Ó Foghludha, *Éigse na Máighe* 121.
114. P. Ua Duinnín, *Amhráin Eoghain Ruaidh Uí Shúilleabháin* 47-48.
115. P. Ua Duinnín, *Amhráin Sheáin Chláraigh Mhic Dhomhnaill* 10: 'The agent of the state often has the hunt on my heels, my shoes are broken and I don't own a penny to mend them.'
116. P. Ua Duinnín, *op. cit.* 51-53.
117. D. de hÍde (An Craoibhín Aoibhinn), *Abhráin agus dánta an Reachtabhraigh* 50: 'Not a word there about a penny in rent nor anything of its kind.'
118. M. Ó Tiomanaidhe, *Abhráin Ghaedhilge an iarthair* 72.
119. S. Ó Ceallaigh, *Filíocht na gCallanán* (Dublin 1967) 60-62.
120. É. Ó Muirgheasa, *Amhráin na Midhe* 20: 'a high price for the goods, that we

might make the rent'.
121. S. Ó Ceallaigh, *Filíocht na gCallanán* 38: 'And you may spend a time drinking since the price of grain increased.'
122. É. Ó Muirgheasa, *Amhráin na Midhe* 19: 'She, Sighle, is ever contending with me since I do task or service for her, for I set no seed nor oats nor flax for her, neither carrots nor beans; think you not, people, that it is I who am wise in not breaking my heart with labour, when so many generous youths would give me 'relief' at Michaelmas feast in the autumn.'
123. *Ibid.*: 'Were I to live and own a herd of cows or a score of sheep, a plough-team or two of fine, young horses like the labourer.'
124. *Op. cit.* 55: 'There are people who covet riches of money and gold, and others who covet wealth of cows and sheep, methinks it would be better to drink a part of each, than to lose the lot when they go under the sod.'
125. S. de Rís, *Peadar Ó Doirnín* 30: 'I will abandon music, fellowship and sport, and set about advancement in this world, I will buy a cow, a horse or two and, maybe, goats and sheep.'
126. D. de híde, *AbhrŒin agus dánta an Reachtabhraigh* 87: 'A fine thing is a dairy-herd and a holding, wheat and barley for reaping, meal in the chest and a fire in the evening and shelter for the travelling man, a shirt and a coat at Mass on a Sunday, a fashionable hat and a coat.'
127. S. Ó Ceallaigh, *Filíocht na gCallanán* 50: 'I would be better off with a horse, a harrow and a plough, a team of yoked and harnessed horses which would set the fields in file. Along with them a dairy-herd was often found, a fire and warmth for a travelling man, generous sustenance, money and yellow gold, people, young and old, with fashionable clothing.'
128. *Op. cit.* 36: 'if you are going to marry . . . go to Seefinn; there is money there and gold, and plenty of matches.'
129. É. Ó Muirgheasa, *Amhráin na Midhe* 66: 'Pól Mac Briain, if you married the hag without money or goods or sheep or cows, my reasoned judgement is that you were out of your wits, seeing that you could be beguiled by a woman without a dowry.'
130. *Op. cit.* 112: 'Were I to have Hanna, I would ask for no dowry with her, and I myself would earn all that we would spend.'
131. Torna, *Seán na Ráithíneach* 341: 'Whoever were promised her in marriage would have a fine agreement, without any dowry in the reckoning in receiving her.'
132. *Op. cit.* 150: 'It is certain that a man would be better off with her, stark-naked, than with a worthless, dried-up detractor with three dowries.' In an interesting word of advice to a young man, the poet advised him: *Faighaidhse ainnir ghlan mhaiseach is pós mar mhnaoi; 'S bíodh roinn mhaith airgid, eallaigh 's óir 'na slighe (op. cit.* 191): 'Find a pure, lovely maiden and wed her as wife and ensure that she has a good portion of money, goods and gold.'
133. *Atá eadtortha araon* in P. Ua Duinnín, *Amhráin Eoghain Ruaidh Uí Shúilleabháin* 77 – a very interesting poem on this theme: 'and whatever were her dowry, I would never claim its half'.
134. D. de híde (An Craoibhín Aoibhinn), *Abhráin agus dánta an Reachtabhraigh* 104: 'And the only fairing I would ask with you is that you and I should be together.' See also *Cnocán Fhaobhair nó Úna Ní Chatháin: 'S nach fear gan misneach dá mhéad a státa nach bpósfadh an stáid-bhean gan pinghin gan bonn (op. cit.* 251), 'and only a man with no spirit, however great his estates, would not marry the lovely lady without penny or coin'.
135. Professor Connell's argument is that the dowry system had existed, but was

45

replaced by 'romantic marriages' in the decades preceding the Famine.

136. S. Ó Ceallaigh, *Filíocht na gCallanán* 45.

137. É. Ó Muirgheasa, *Amhráin na Midhe* 53-54: 'Neither do I see the sheep bleating on the fair plains, nor horses being trained after hounds going over the hedges . . . neither tubers nor roots nor any other novelty to come on the scene, but when August comes, a potatoe-gathering dug with a spade. I do not see the meat in joints being sold in the stalls, I do not see the threshed barley or wheat, nor a pea- or bean-stalk for it is not of their nature to grow in your land . . . I do not see the undamaged stooks in your haggard at the feast of St John, nor do I see the 'pattern' days that we were wont to have by the Boyne.'

138. *Op. cit.* 141: 'were it not for my being stout and corpulent from eating meat, I would walk with you part of the way to show you the road'.

139. É. Ó Muirgheasa, *Amhráin Airt Mhic Chubhthaigh agus amhráin eile* i 43-44: 'The Ulstermen who are wont to be tired and listless, returning lifelessly from Meath, they visit Ó Duilleachán's hostelry at night . . . I soon hear from the youths coming back, returning from their autumnal visit.'

140. R. Ó Foghludha, *Eoghan Ruadh Ó Súilleabháin* 147: 'he thought it a luxury to get potatoes and dregs of buttermilk'.

141. D. Ó Donnchú, *Filíocht Mháire Bhuidhe Ní Laoghaire* 49: 'who ever deserved to get honour and respect; bright generous rooms and herds of cattle yielding milk, well-renowned women in their houses who would dispense abundance of bread'.

142. See n. 43 and text above.

143. P. Ua Duinnín, *Amhráin Eoghain Ruaidh Uí Shúilleabháin* 72.

144. D. de hÍde (An Craoibhín Aoibhinn), *Abhráin agus dánta an Reachtabhraigh* 171.

145. *Op. cit.* 254: 'There is not a weaver or hatter, cobbler or tailor, from Lough Carn river to Loughrea, neither nail-maker, blacksmith, tradesman nor oarmaker whose heart it (whiskey) would not raise.'

146. *Op. cit.* 259: 'A streetful of boys who dine and sleep along with him, it is Seán who gives them work and good pay accordingly.'

147. P. Ua Duinnín *Amhráin Eoghain Ruaidh Uí Shúilleabháin* 54: 'I will not stop until I make my way to Galway with my spade, where I will get my sixpence and breakfast each day as wages.'

148. É. Ó Muirgheasa, *Amhráin na Midhe* 113: 'Would I not be better off with a workman who would go forth as a labourer and give me his wages at the end of each day, or with an idling tramp who would carry his bag and share with my children what charity he would collect, than with the like of you . . . '.

POSTSCRIPT

The Gaelic literature of the eighteenth century exists in a remarkably rich form, often indeed in the very hand of its composers, and where it survives in copies made by contemporaries or near-contemporaries it gives an arresting and unique idea of the diffusion of ideas and contacts in time and space in the Gaelic world of the period. It was a world which would not have been unfamiliar in medieval Europe, but which was unparalleled elsewhere by the eighteenth century. Most other surviving early languages were already reduced to little more than the level of patois, with no written literature, and with little participation or patronage from the upper classes. Irish on the other hand had a vigorous literature recorded and disseminated in manuscript form, and enjoyed patronage from the upper classes some of whom themselves had pretensions to scholarship or poetic talent.

Patronage was vital to this process, and indeed the division between rural patrons and the urban world, and between Gaelic society and English society, which was a hindrance to development in some ways, also served as a protective mantle of its rich but archaic characteristics. One can of course exaggerate the value of patronage. It was more widespread of literate men in their role of transcribers and tutors than as poets. Indeed, poets were a minority among these literate men, and as literacy spread in the eighteenth century must have accounted for a sharply declining proportion.

Patronage itself declined or deteriorated over the eighteenth century in a way which reflects not simply the decline in the fortunes of archaic patrons but the diffusion of literacy which subtly altered the potential role of patronage itself. In fact, it shifted decisively from patronage of poets as such to the transcription of manuscripts and to tutoring and teaching: for the potential patron the value of poetic talent and of the skills of transcribing documents or teaching literacy had been reversed.[1] In other words poets survived less because of their poetic talents than because of their other skills; poetry itself attracted less and less patronage, and it became a by-product of the leisure of transcribers and teachers, and of a handful of independent comfortable large farmers. Indeed, the latter category disappeared quickly after mid-century. Seán Clárach MacDomhnaill and Piaras Mac Gearailt in Limerick and Cork respectively; and in Clare, Micheál Ó Coimín and Seán Ó hUaithnín, must have been virtually its last representatives. Fresh instances do not come readily to mind for the second half of the century. The teachers themselves were in an extraordinary position: they practised the arts and the culture of the past for a growingly private world, while they made their living increasingly by imparting literacy in English. They thus stood quite literally in two worlds.

In a fresh look at the Hidden Ireland, politicization would merit more attention than it received in my 1969 paper. It is reflected in the poetry and in the manuscripts though in a diffuse and frequently ambiguous manner. The abjuration oath in 1709, the execution of James Cotter in 1720 (which led to a remarkable response among Cò. Cork poets), the tragic deaths of Morty Oge O'Sullivan in 1754 and Art Ó Laoghaire in 1773, or the execution of Nicholas Sheehy in 1766, are all reflected in the poetry of the century. While the aisling itself is meaningless as a political message, some of the poetry does have a sense of political realities or aspirations that revolved around contemporary events. Seán Ó Murchadha's *Tá an bhliadhain seo ag teacht* in 1744 is the most significant of these poems referring as the poems rarely do not to diffuse hopes but to the aspirations prompted by specific preparations on the continent for invasion. We are almost listening to the conversations in some circles in Munster, in effect to the loose talk which alarmed Protestants in Cork or Clare, the two great counties of literary composition in Irish. The Clare Grand Jury arraigned Seán Ó hUaithnín in 1748 for the sentiments expressed in a poem. Micheál Ó Coimín appeared on his behalf and himself wrote a Jacobite poem as late as 1755.[2] The Seven Years War (1756-63) was reflected in the poetry, notably in that of Liam Inglis, who expressed Jacobite sentiments: with him any meaningful expression of Jacobite aspiration dies.

The alliterative device of using planter names in poems is largely a poetic device (the same was done with Catholic notables), but it is significant that the names of John Bagwell and Thomas Maude in Tipperary crop up in several of the poems using this device. They are a comment on the Tipperary events which culminated in Sheehy's death. They are, therefore, a political comment, less on

48

the so-called planter class than on a party, the hard-line Protestants of Munster, in the momentous years of the 1760s. In a sense the poetry opens up a hidden political world, not the world of oppression and poverty described by Corkery, but a world in which some of the images have well-defined political connotations, and the light-and-shade in the poetry reflects the shifts in political consciousness that were taking place at the time. In a shadowy fashion, something of a process of modernization can be detected in the poetry, or more accurately in the mentalities of those who wrote it.

Precisely because patronage had deteriorated in quality, that is, that a common mental world was no longer shared by poet and patron, the poets were freer and more able to express ideas of their own. There was a shift on the part of patrons from support of ideas held in common with the poets to mere purchase of what were regarded increasingly as antiquarian manuscripts. Micheál Og Ó Longáin for instance was to a large extent a commissioned transcriber dependent on a clientele with whom he had limited social or intellectual communication. This left such men free to cultivate political ideas of their own. The aisling had been disavowed by Piaras Mac Gearailt in the 1760s: this was something of a rejection of the old world with its backward-looking patrons and its Jacobite overtones. Significantly he both rejected the Jacobite ideal, and wove Maude and Bagwell, two of the main protagonists of Tipperary anti-Catholic activities in the 1760s, into his alliteration. The decline of patronage left poets free to pursue their own ideas, ultimately to become more radical and to absorb the new political ideas expressed by the United Irishmen and Defenders. There is little difference on this score between the poets Ó Longáin in Cork and Riocard Bairéad on the Mullet peninsula in Mayo, and Laurence O'Connor the schoolmaster leader of the Meath Defenders in the mid-1790s.

These changes emphasize just how archaic Eoghan Rua Ó Súilleabháin was: his aislings all come from the 1770s when the political mentality of the poets at large had radically changed, and reflect something of an intellectual timewarp. He moved of course along a corridor running from the east Kerry border down the Blackwater to Mallow, in which despite the massive turnover of property in the seventeenth century little pockets of comfortable Catholics survived, notably around Monaminy in the shadow of the

Nagle mountains. Indeed, Ó Súilleabháin had served one household of the Nagles as a tutor, and his poetry has many references to the Mallow region or hints of it. The very fact that a poet could have such a Jacobite character as Ó Súilleabháin in his aislings in a region of comfortable Catholics like the Hennessys and the Nagles is of course a reminder that a gulf had emerged between the poet and the class that would formerly have been his patrons. Neither the Nagles nor the Hennessys at or near Monaminy shared his political outlook as far as we know, and indeed in the 1790s while the United Irishmen spread in parts of Cork and included Miceál Óg Ó Longáin in their number, they failed to a remarkable degree to attract any of the comfortable Catholics not simply of Cork but of Munster at large. The gulf between patron and poet had become a wide and unbridgeable one if indeed a link between the two survived at all. Interesting too as a reflection of changes is how the death of Art Ó Laoghaire attracted no laments by established poets, and how the one lament on his death existed only in oral tradition. The poetic and transcribing mechanism of recording the fortunes of the Gaelic upper class had palpably broken down by the 1770s in the bleak lands between Millstreet and Macroom.

Patronage, such as it was in its survival, was greatly debased, patronising indeed in the modern pejorative sense of the term. Much of it came from urban sources, little different whether Protestant or, like Bishop Murphy's collecting of manuscripts in early nineteenth-century Cork, Catholic. In such a climate transcribing activity could not only survive but thrive in the towns, as in the interesting Seán Ó Neachtain circle in Dublin. The Dublin patronage of the scribal activity of Muiris Ó Gormáin is a facet of this activity in its new-found character. Charles O'Conor, though keeping his own diary in Irish, essentially directed his public activity to preserving the record of the past. Indeed in the face of this fashionable and antiquarian interest around them, the poets regarded themselves as antiquarians, as in the revealing 'Failte Sheoin Lloyd roimhe na Antiquarians chum Innis ChluonRam(h)ad, ait agus innod mar thionnsgladar Collaiste Gaoidhilge beith acudh.'[3]

The survival of a literature in Irish in purely manuscript form is quite extraordinary. In one sense the absence of printing is a reflection of the failure of patronage: even urban patronage was not interested in printing, seeing the literature merely as an antiquarian record to be preserved through love of the past or simply as an antiquarian pursuit. John Lloyd wrote his description of Clare in English in 1780.[4] What printing existed was largely of material which had an oral context for its dissemination: some sermons, Butler's catechism in 1792, and a decade later in Clonmel the religious poems of Tadhg Gaelach Ó Súilleabháin. In Cork the interest in publication in Irish came from Micheál Og Ó Longáin, but it came to nought as a result of the lack of real interest among his patrons.

Corkery's Hidden Ireland centres on Cork and Kerry. In some ways the most interesting literary world of eighteenth-century Ireland, at any rate in the second half of the century, was in Clare. Not only Merriman's justly famous poem but Lloyd's call, even if in antiquarian form, for a 'College' in 1780 point to the vigour of its Gaelic society at a time when the Gaelic culture of Cork and Kerry had already decidedly passed its peak. Lloyd's proposal of a Gaelic College or society had been made well before 1800; elsewhere, in Limerick or Cork, it appeared only after that date. Less of the Clare poetry has been published and its society is more of a closed book. Corkery did not really appreciate that Clare culturally was part of Munster, not Connaught as he suggested.[5] The fact that schoolmasters migrated more to Clare from Limerick than in the reverse direction (Lloyd being the best instance) also illustrates the vitality of the region. Lloyd's entrepreneurial move into publication, albeit in English, in 1780 was itself one dimension of that, an unusual one for a poet-schoolmaster in rural Ireland. Several of Clare's poets had been gentry or of gentry background. The county had a substantial class of small rustic gentry who survived into the nineteenth century and of which we get a glimpse in Dutton's picture of the county's leisured class, with incomes from £100 to £500 p.a., lounging in the streets or in the coffee house of Ennis.[6] This little world, a closed if not exactly a hidden one, remains fascinating, and indeed awaits investigation in depth. Clearly it must have had both intellectual and social qualities to account for its survival when other districts were on the wane. Its strengths ensured too that its antiquarians, and they were now antiquarians more than poets, made a mark in the Gaelic studies of the early nineteenth century: there were two Claremen, Theophilus Ó Flanagáin and Padraigh Ó Loinsigh, in the first Gaelic society in Dublin in 1807.[7]

The Hidden Ireland has been an influential book, impressive indeed in the durability of its appeal. The title itself was of course a singularly apt one, not only accurately summarizing the author's approach, but having an intrinsic appeal suggesting access to a secret world beyond the historical documents.[8] The abiding impression from the book however is the narrow source base of the author. From preconceived ideas he read the readily accessible poets, and informed his historical opinions with impressions drawn from a tiny handful of authors: essentially his historical reading is listed on p.10 of the work. Apart from the authors mentioned there, almost the only historical source cited is J. M. Calwell's book. Even Lecky is usually referred to only in general terms and the reader's impression is that Corkery probably read him rather cursorily. Froude is significantly not included in the list, and his name crops up in the text only once (and elsewhere in a sole footnote). The book was written from set ideas about Irish history and the Irish condition, and the poetry itself is interpreted or manipulated to fit into that context.[9] It is written with great enthusiasm, and despite verging on the sentimental its quality is infectious. However, the confidence with which the book's opinions and judgements are conveyed suggests that the state of Gaelic Ireland was clear-cut, and it may thereby have discouraged the urge to look into that society or its mentality any further. Yet, given the nature of the Gaelic poetry and the many currents in it, it is doubtful if any more remarkable evidence exists in Europe of the intellectual, social and political recesses of an important and influential layer of society – essentially a middling group – in the rural world.

NOTES

1. L. M. Cullen, 'Patrons, teachers and literacy in Irish 1700-1850', paper read at conference on literacy and language in Ireland, 1700-1900, University College, Dublin, May 1983.

2. L. M. Cullen, 'Catholics under the penal laws', *Eighteenth-century Ireland*, vol. 1 (1986), p.32.

3. Maynooth College, MS 3A18, p.21.

4. *A short tour, or an impartial and accurate description of the county of Clare, with some particular and historical observations* (Ennis, 1780).

5. D. Corkery, *The hidden Ireland* (1956 ed.), p.249.

6. H. Dutton, *Statistical survey of the county of Clare* (Dublin, 1808), pp.299-300.

7. J. E. Caerwyn Williams and M. Ní Mhuiríosa, *Traidisiún liteartha na nGael* (Dublin, 1979), p.319.

8. John Horgan (NIHE, Dublin) has told me that he had it on good authority that the actual title had been suggested by the publisher.

9. For two views, very different from one another, on Corkery's work, see S. O Tuama, 'Donall O Corcora', and B. O'Buachalla, 'O Corcora agus an Hidden Ireland', *Scríobh*, vol. 4 (1979), ed. S. O Mordha.

FURTHER READING

Corkery, Daniel. *The Fortunes of the Irish Language* (Mercier Press, Cork, 1968).

—— *The Hidden Ireland: A Study of Gaelic Munster in the Eighteenth Century* (1925) (Gill and Macmillan, Dublin, 1967).

—— *Synge and Anglo-Irish Literature* (1931) (Mercier Press, Cork, 1966).

Cullen, L. M. *The Emergence of Modern Ireland 1600-1900* (Batsford, London, 1981).

Ó Buachalla, Breandán. *I mBéal Feirste Cois Cuain* (An Clochomhair, Baile Átha Cliath, 1968).

Ó Tuama, Seán. 'Donal Ó Corcora agus Filíocht na Gaeilge' *Studia Hibernica* no 5 (1965), pp. 29-41.

Saul, George Brandon. *Daniel Corkery* (Bucknell University Press, Lewisburg, 1975).